CYBERNETICS OF GHOSTS

Editor: Michael Salu

Line Editor: Hannah Gregory
Second Line Editor: Rebecca Bligh

Publisher: James Ginzburg

Design: Monika Janulevičiūtė and Kareem Lotfy

First published 2024 by Subtext / Multiverse LTD
10 Park Street
Bristol
BS1 5HX, UK
Subtextbooks.net

ISBN 978-1-919601-53-3
Copyright © Multiverse LTD and the authors

The right of each author to be identified as the author of their work has been asserted in accordance with the Copyright, Designs and Patents Act 1988.

With gratitude to Gabriel Gbadamosi, WritersMosaic and Akin Akinwumi.

CYBERNETICS OF GHOSTS

Index

Introduction Michael Salu	**8**
Ghosts of a Third Mandy-Suzanne Wong	**26**
Voice of the First Metre Kelly Krumrie	**42**
The Lucy Temerlin Institute for Broken Shapeshifters Resident #4: Shanthi/Brad Kuzhali Manickavel	**54**
Lettera 22 ∀i	**70**
Toucan and Jaguar Lisa Hsiao Chen	**92**
The Ghost of the Apricot Geoffrey Morrison	**106**
Brittle Paper Innocent Chizaram Ilo	**120**
More Life Rion Amilcar Scott	**134**

When Viewed From the Head Rather Than the Foot Simon Okotie	150
Amnesiac Beach Fire Andrea Mason	164
Patients Is a Virtual Iphgenia Baal	180
Soprano machine They are in Palmers Green and someone is about to be — Tice Cin	196
Bedlam and Its Buffers Steve Barbaro	214
The Once-girl Made of Mycelium Shingai Kagunda	226
Repeating Program Blake Butler	240
Biographies	252

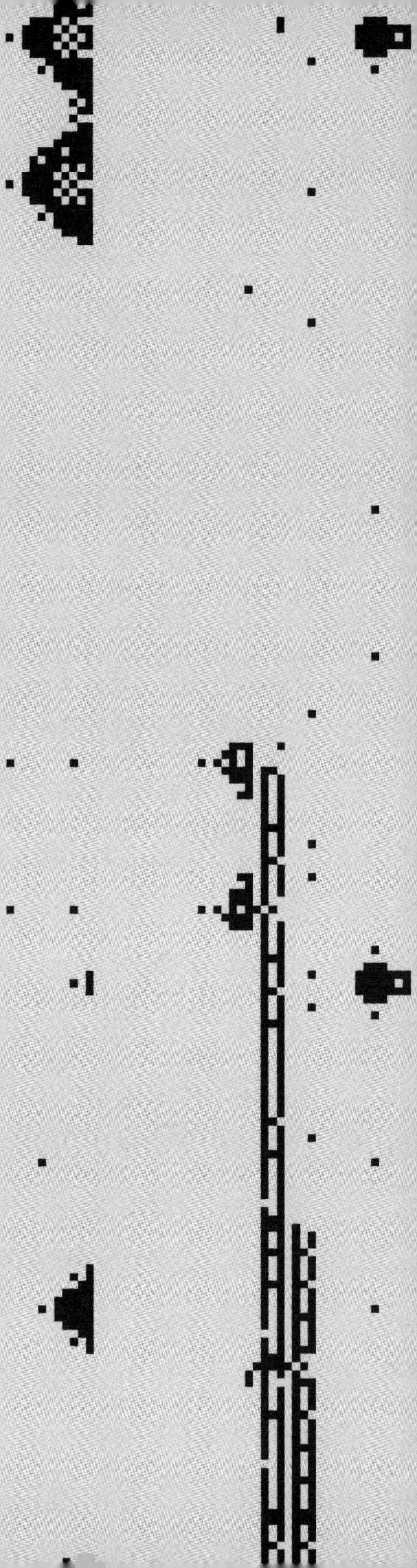

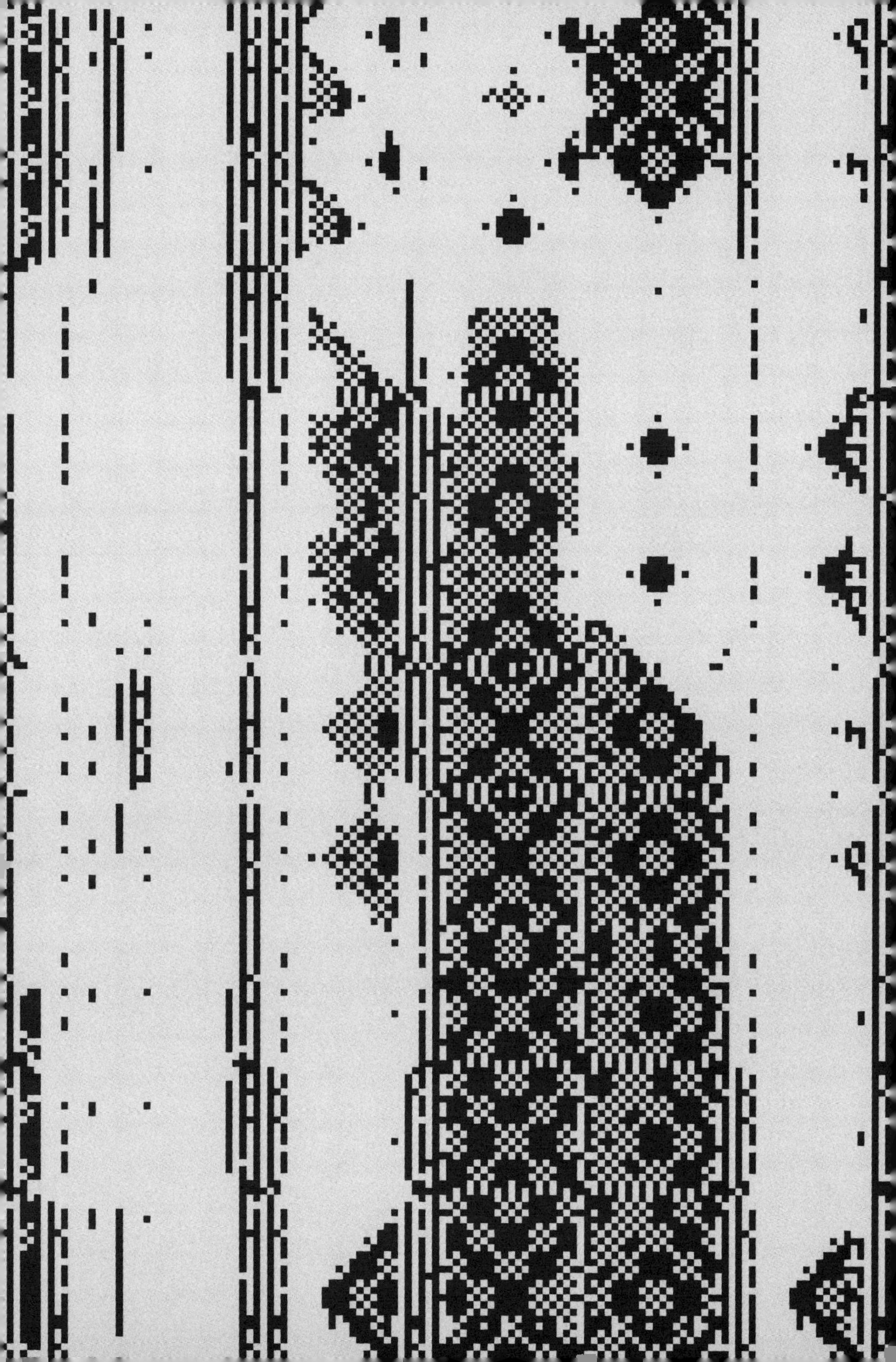

Introduction

Michael Salu

You could see this collection of original stories as a networked artwork, as a series of independent but connected nodes orbiting a central node. This central node has already been solidified by its occurrence in the past and will be solidified further by how time allows for evidence to accumulate and for archival forms of memory. This evidence gathering across time mirrors the data structures of machine-learning models for aspirational 'artificial intelligence', which process the data of past happenings, from the living and the dead, to inform both who we should be and what we should do tomorrow.

This node – the conceit at the anthology's heart – is a lecture by novelist and essayist Italo Calvino, 'Cybernetics and Ghosts', which he presented across Italy in 1967 and later published in his essay collection *The Literature Machine* (1987). Cognizant of our diminishing reliance on the enigmatic might of an indeterminate spirit world and our increasing dependence on determinate statistical methods (established from subjective origins), the rapid progress computational linguistics was making at the time, and Darwinian categorization, Calvino playfully and presciently riffed on what the human author's future could look like once machines, or computers, became sophisticated enough to offer writing comparable to that of humans. A tantalizing premise, but Calvino's provocation doesn't rest on sensationalism; rather he proposes an opportunity for irreverent intellectual exploration. As he pondered the growing influence of computational linguistics, a discipline geared to making human language comprehensible to computers through code, it was natural for him to simultaneously look beyond and into the past to consider the origins and importance of storytelling, if not with an anthropologist's rigour, then with the creative licence afforded a curious mind. He comes to hypothesize that having navigated the canons of human experience, a literature machine will eventually aim for classicism. A machine, he reasonably speculates, would lean towards ordered forms of language and communication: long-established tropes, systems and narrative formulas. In the face of his prediction becoming a norm, what of today's human author? How do they think about their tailored intimacy with machine?

Digital infrastructure has defined our lives for the best part of four decades, and, depending on when you were born, your relationship with, let's call it, the *computational entity* will differ immensely. Each year, societal, geopolitical and even biological instances (such as pandemics), pull us further into spatial and cognitive bionic synchronicity with machines; from protein sequencing to CRISPR gene editing, our bodies are subject to more and more mathematical optimization. The ravages of war offer new technology-driven economic opportunities. Social upheaval enables increasingly granular technological imposition, evident in how the codebases of digital services are adjusted to increase users' dependence, and noticeable in the tightening grip of surveillance capitalism. Here, functions like facial recognition and algorithmic discrimination both penalize and utilize dissenting behaviour and deviations from what is considered 'humanist' — according to established categories of race, class and gender — in order to maintain society's economic order.

New challenges unleashed by a 'changing environment' (changed by who?) require expedient solutions to help us survive. Robotics make rapid gains towards dominating labour and production, feeding and learning the minutiae of our daily banalities. What we've known and understood as culture — namely films, books, music, and even the proxy for feudal society that sport can be — becomes a hieroglyphic vernacular through which we communicate, and for our computational guides — our Hades, if you like — to deepen their influence. Slow-motion video. Automated subtitling. Reimagining the stanza. The hero narrative governing much of our entertainment, where you are meant to aspire to be the main character, reducing all others to listless NPCs (Non-Player Characters). The iridescent irreverence of memes that often demand the viewer have some awareness of a cultural motif, and if not make haste to seek it out, to prevent being left behind by a viral swarm. We're passively yet twitchily primed for optimal engagement within this semiotic swirl. The virtual public sphere is rendered with a cinematic grammar that regales and encourages us into interactive contemporary folktales where we unconsciously utilize imbibed storytelling techniques aligned with structured statistical methodologies to guide more manageable binary perspectives and ideas. Here, everything uttered becomes fiction due to the economic priorities of the worlds to which we commit our words, where both worlds and words live, grow and shift in meaning. Inevitably, lore from the same films, books, art and music becomes fuel to feed the fires of automation, where congealed masses of ideas envelope the mythological taxonomies we have used to understand each other until now, mainly within the framework of a dominant epistemology.

Observe how distant the vanguards of our cultural mythologies have become from the reins guiding our 'progress', a responsibility now left to technological demigods whose dexterity with code often appears at odds with the sublimity to which art has traditionally aspired. Sci-fi novels, dystopian warnings embedded, become manifestos rather than notes of caution. Literature, as a machine in its own right, remains at the time of writing relatively indifferent to the vernacular of digital realms, be they those of internet delirium or computer vision's reconstitution of physical time and space. There are many 'internet novels', but they rarely depart from corporeal primacy. Yes, we have science fiction: with *Neuromancer* (1986), William Gibson gave us a toolkit for thinking about how we might understand digital life. Octavia Butler's *Kindred* (1979) offered a way to think about instantaneous movement between dimensions. But arguably, there is insufficient contemporary creative writing that wholly inhabits the virtual consciousness as a norm, away from the authorial 'I'.

What does collective memory look like from the inside of the cognitive experiences of digital life, and its many psychological rollercoasters? How might what we still understand as literature engage our non-linear adventures in the digital everyday? Like when, say, you shift from a video of an ex-lover charting their battle with cancer to, within milliseconds, a passive-aggressive WhatsApp message from an intrusive boss, to a video of a man punching a monkey, to a banking app to pay your ballooning rent or mortgage, all while following instructions to cross an intersection in a 'smart city'. What do the whispering trails of all this information become as one moves between these interactive, ever-learning channels of life? There's a brutal and visceral pulling of one's consciousness when using a smartphone, as if dropping through a membranous portal, a quick removal from any surrounding flesh-and-blood company, to become a kind of meat-ghost until this borrowed soul manages to return. However one wants to deem this realm, the virtual space plays an imprecise yet undeniable role in our synthesis of the world. Rather than the wonder of geology, flora and fauna, the digital realm is, principally, a capitalist creation, which must progress a certain way, with specific interests, and appears evermore indifferent to our need to find poetry in the awe of living.

Of course, the relationship between poet and scientist is an age-old antagonism. 'Cursed, cursed creator! Why did I live? Why, in that instant, did I not extinguish the spark of existence you had so wantonly bestowed?' laments the 'monster', Victor Frankenstein's notorious invention, in Mary Shelley's *Frankenstein*, first published in 1818. A revelation hits the monster: the world of 'man' will never grant him grace, acceptance, love, or any comprehension of his poetic sensitivity due to his horrific appearance, and his *unnaturalness*. Science, and more specifically in our case, computer science, winds around the laws of nature and being (as they have been understood thus far), prophesying salvation from our destruction. Meanwhile poetry remains wilfully elusive, slipping forwards, trying to recalibrate its voice and vision. Once central to societal and even technological discourse, literature's diminishing influence is related to a widening science-poetry chasm. Humanities departments face closure, governments steer students towards STEM subjects for cyber protection and strategic positioning in a more diffused hierarchical global economy. It is as if there is a lessening need for the individual to think critically, uniquely or empathetically. This moment in time brings to mind Stanisław Lem's story 'Non Serviam' (one of his reviews of non-existent books collected in A *Perfect Vacuum*, 1971), in which mathematically constructed 'personoids', created by a fictional scientist, can mimic human behaviour and interactions, but only on a linguistic level, as they are devoid of human fragility and fallibility, and therefore do not feel, or think, as we do, and are immune to alarm, confusion and distress.

The fraught relationship between science and poetry is central to Calvino's cybernetic thought experiment. He encourages us to muse on how humans first strung sounds together to express a need or emotion. How we drew and painted scenes and stories to process and memorialize happenings with developing sophistication, until we arrived at a series of discrete elements: words, concepts or rules. Through combination, these elements evolved into a code for interpreting the world. Discretion, in this mathematical sense, as Calvino uses it, implies a structure with distinct constituent parts or values. Calvino's questionable implication here is that we differ from sky, sea, fowl or dirt. Such technical analyses might irk the poet, who attempts to dance with the phenomena of the sublime, which remains elusive to poet and scientist alike. Calvino knew this only too well: in response to his own provocation, he sardonically suggests that he desires a discrete system to one day relieve him of poetic responsibility and liberate him from his fear of the unknown or uncertain. The vectors for the system or code — namely, words, in infinite combinations — present ways for us to tell stories, describe our experiences and accumulate what we understand as meaning, further sedimenting through layers upon layers of lived application, to eventually form metaphors.

In his book *I Am a Strange Loop* (2007), American cognitive scientist Douglas Hofstadter uses metaphor to great effect, deploying real-world experiences of life and death to discuss how to mathematically measure whether a 'soul' could live on beyond a human body, through the externalization of 'secondary memories'. This process would occur through the objects a person, now deceased, had scribbled notes on, or via the stories they had told and the lives they had impacted. Traces of memories as little fragments of soul flicker through the world, like tiny embers, to become part of collective life, shared by and with others; these soul fragments endure as a mathematically reducible equation. Literature has long had a similar function — as this anthology pointedly demonstrates — connecting us through ideas, memories and experiences, interlinking our references, with one work leading to another to make contact with others across time, unhindered by death. Our data-laden computational world demonstrates another emerging evolution of this collective consciousness.

Metaphor remains essential to technological advancement. On the one hand, technologists employ metaphors to support the maths used to determine future realities, and on the other, metaphors can serve as crude branded frontispieces to obfuscate extractive intent. Take Google's appropriation of the name and storied legacy of West African writer and abolitionist Olaudah Equiano. To narrativize the company's undersea data pipeline, which runs from western Europe down the West coast of Africa, unironically retracing transatlantic slave routes, Google called its new infrastructure 'Equiano', and even recalled his story as an airless marketing metaphor. Equiano was a formerly enslaved person who contributed through his work to overturning the dehumanization of chattel slavery and its semantic legacy.

A whirlpool of feedback loops embeds metaphor in our digital unconscious; the weight of this mechanization of myth attempts to command the poetic imagination's submission to a statistical reality, to ensure cognitive pliability for techno-futures. We're now well aware of algorithmic computing's influence on societal function and formulation, where models intuit and develop patterns of action and content, currently based on probabilistic methods (but with the vastness of quantum computing in ascendence), which guides us into a frictionless sameness. One can imagine, or arguably already witness, a coalescing mimesis of the self or the collective self. Twentieth-century anthropologist René Girard suggested a 'mimetic theory', whereby human imitation is inevitable and, over time, erodes differences among demarcated sets of people. Mimesis means we will all desire the same things, says Girard, which will only lead to fervent rivalry. This rivalry causes a third party to be made to serve as a sacrificial scapegoat, in an attempt to maintain peace within society, but this peace is doomed to be temporary: ultimately violence between mimetic rivals will prevail.

᯾

What would the experimental literary collective Oulipo have created if they were formed not in the 1960s, but in the 2020s? Contemporary to Calvino and also mentioned in his 'Cybernetics and Ghosts' lecture, after which he was invited to join, Oulipo was founded by French novelist Raymond Queneau and chemical engineer François Le Lionnais, and involved both writers and mathematicians. They revelled in using mathematical metaphors as creative constraints for writing. One can draw a faint line from the group's interest in the potential of early data analysis methods and linguistic interpretations to the processes behind generative art, where variables and sequences are tweaked to shift information and visual criteria across digital canvases, node-based interfaces and the timelines of media software.

We have approached this anthology with a playful, Oulipo-like spirit. Its interconnected structure, with Calvino's essay as the central node, was our only constraint – in some ways, like a classic creative writing exercise. I asked each writer to read the essay and respond with a work of fiction. Beyond this, our contributors – invited because of their adeptness at thinking variously across the intangibles of contemporary myth – were free to interpret the 'Cybernetics and Ghosts' text however they liked. Their responses have been fascinating to witness. Serendipitous connections form between ideas, with each writer exploring a different aspect of Calvino's essay, with grounded speculation about how our myths and metaphors are transformed in tightening embrace with machines. As

Oulipo well knew, artistic expression, especially that of the collective, can benefit from a measure of constraint.

This work of collective storytelling brings to mind another significant Oulipo contributor, George Perec. His novel *Life, a User's Manual* (1978) weaves together narratives of lives according to a system of rules based on puzzle games, set within the larger spatial constraint of an apartment block. Everyone you'll read in the pages of this anthology shares such a communal space, and is free to come and go as they like. Raymond Queneau's story *Exercises in Style* (1947) is another example of how generative methods can be applied to writing. Queneau writes several versions of a bus journey; in each telling he calls upon a linguistic, sensory or mathematical variable in order to switch between the perspectives of the passengers and styles of language. In *Cybernetics, or Ghosts?*, you'll meet unruly variables from fifteen authors of different dispositions, minds and locations around the world, with different life experiences. Monika Janulevičiūtė and Kareem Lotfy's generative design adds another conscious element. The designers have reimagined early weaving technologies, developing a modular scheme and using software to create a series of sequential patterns through the book — a distinct and beautiful visual contribution to this dialogue. The collection intertwines the threads that make up living and being: the stories, the experiences, the memories, and the ways machines become yet another metaphor for the human condition. I'm eternally grateful to the brilliance of Hannah Gregory, Rebecca Bligh and James Ginzburg, the creative and intellectual generosity of our contributors, and the deeply considered stories they have unearthed, which remind us of the enigmatic nature of the imagination. Assembly-line production of the written word, Calvino suggests, will be comfortably replaced, which frees us to think with the complex histories of story, fable and myth, and makes room, we hope, for anthologies like this.

15

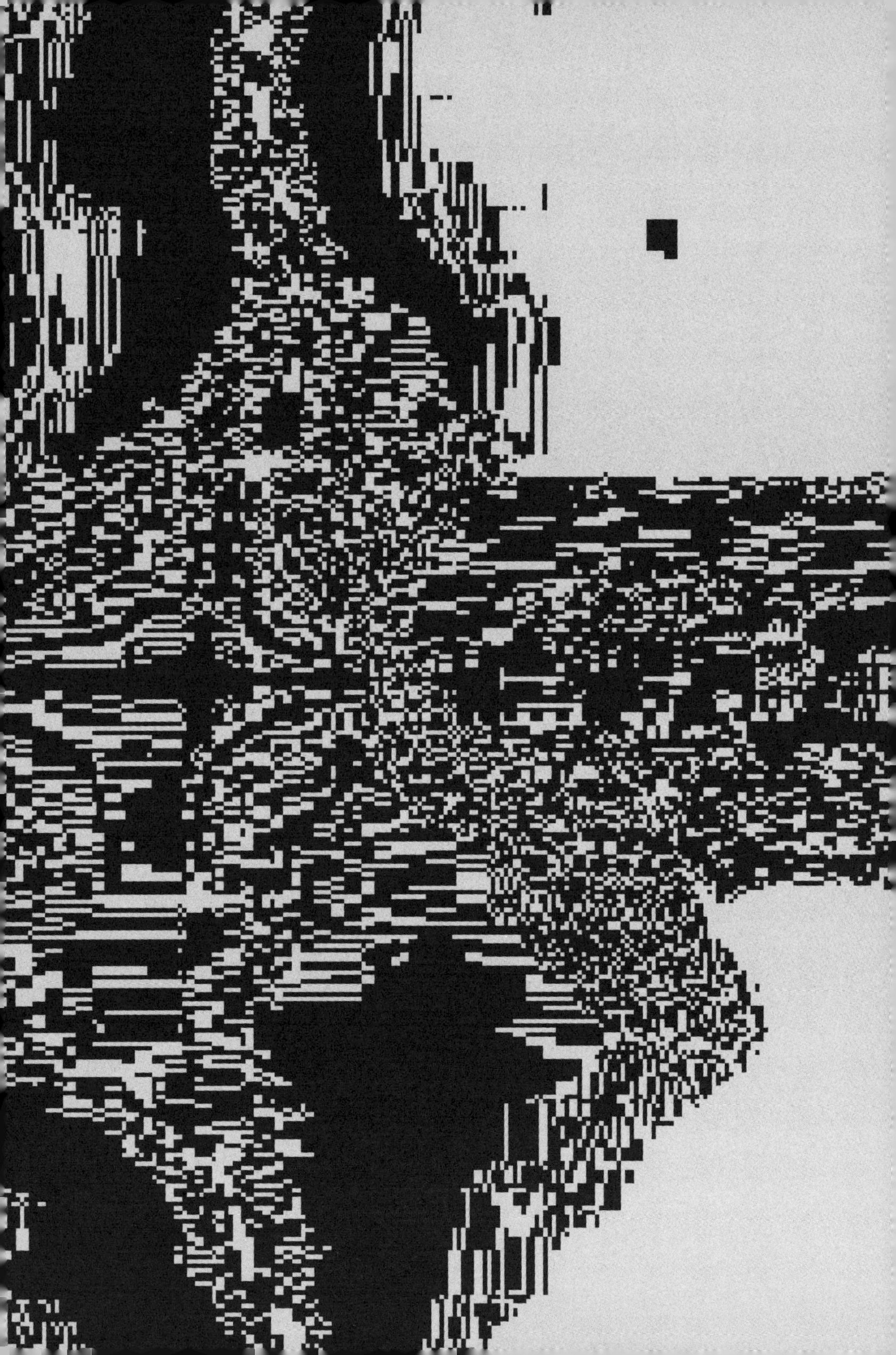

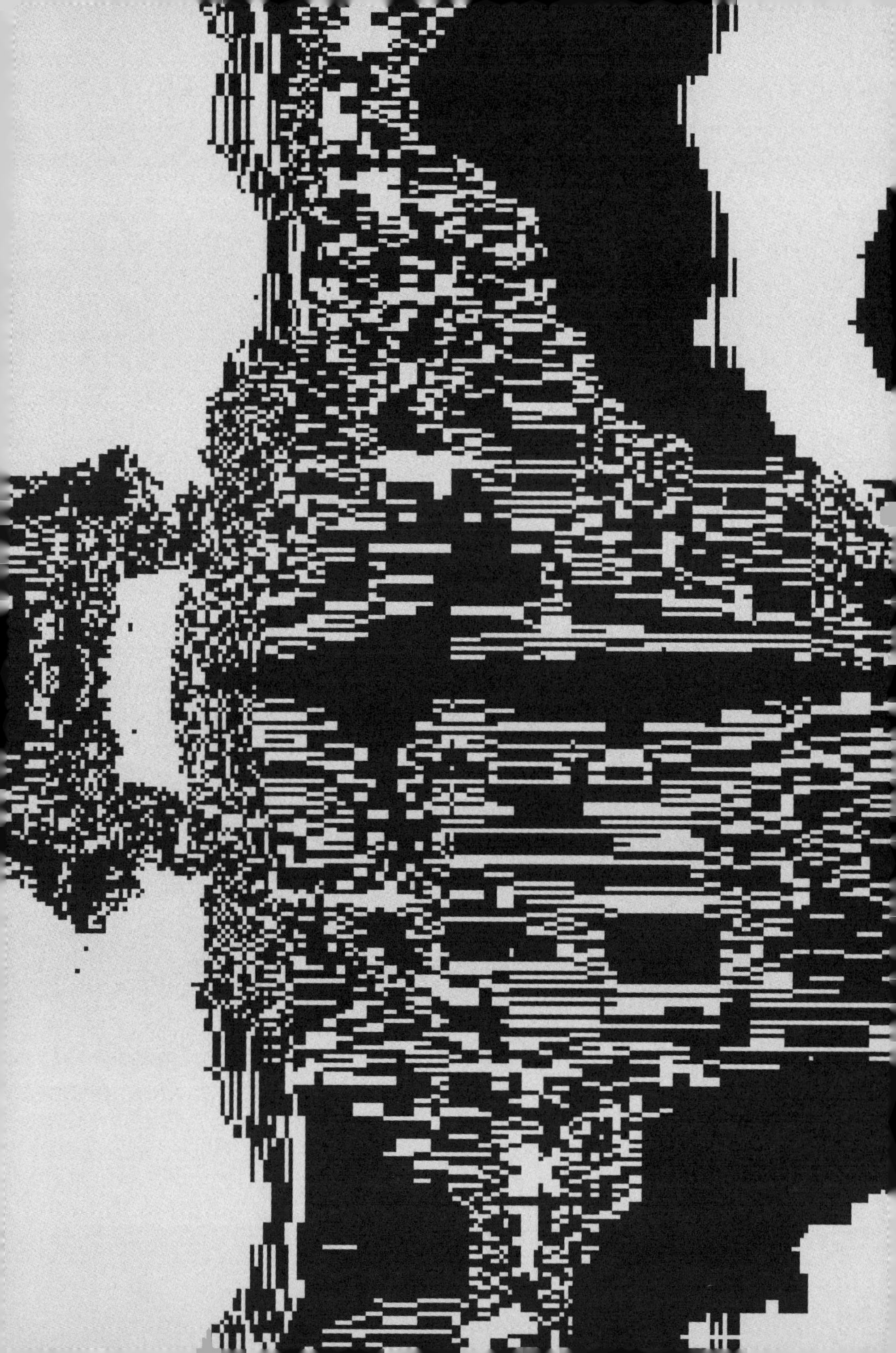

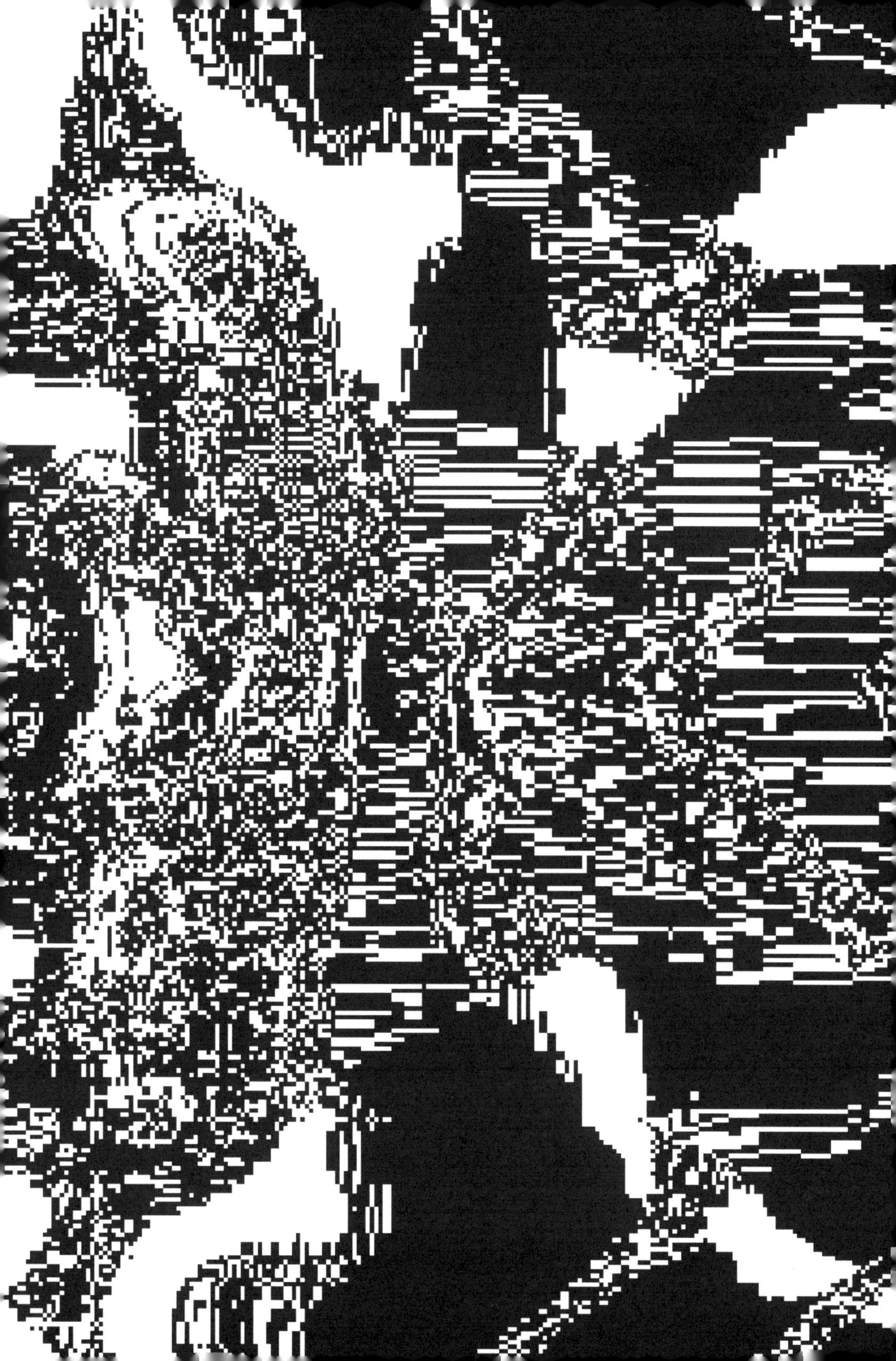

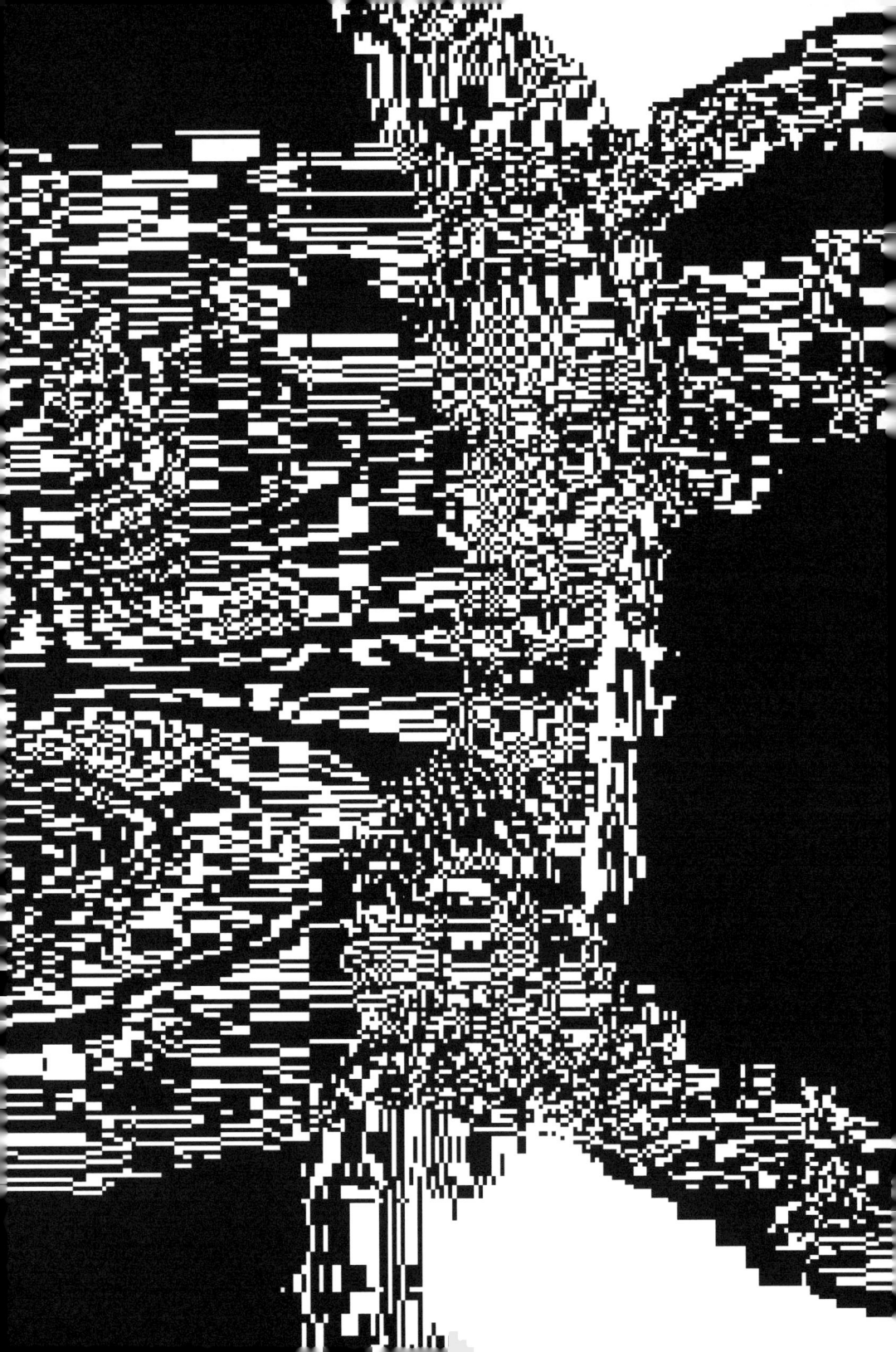

GHOST AT MANDY'S WE

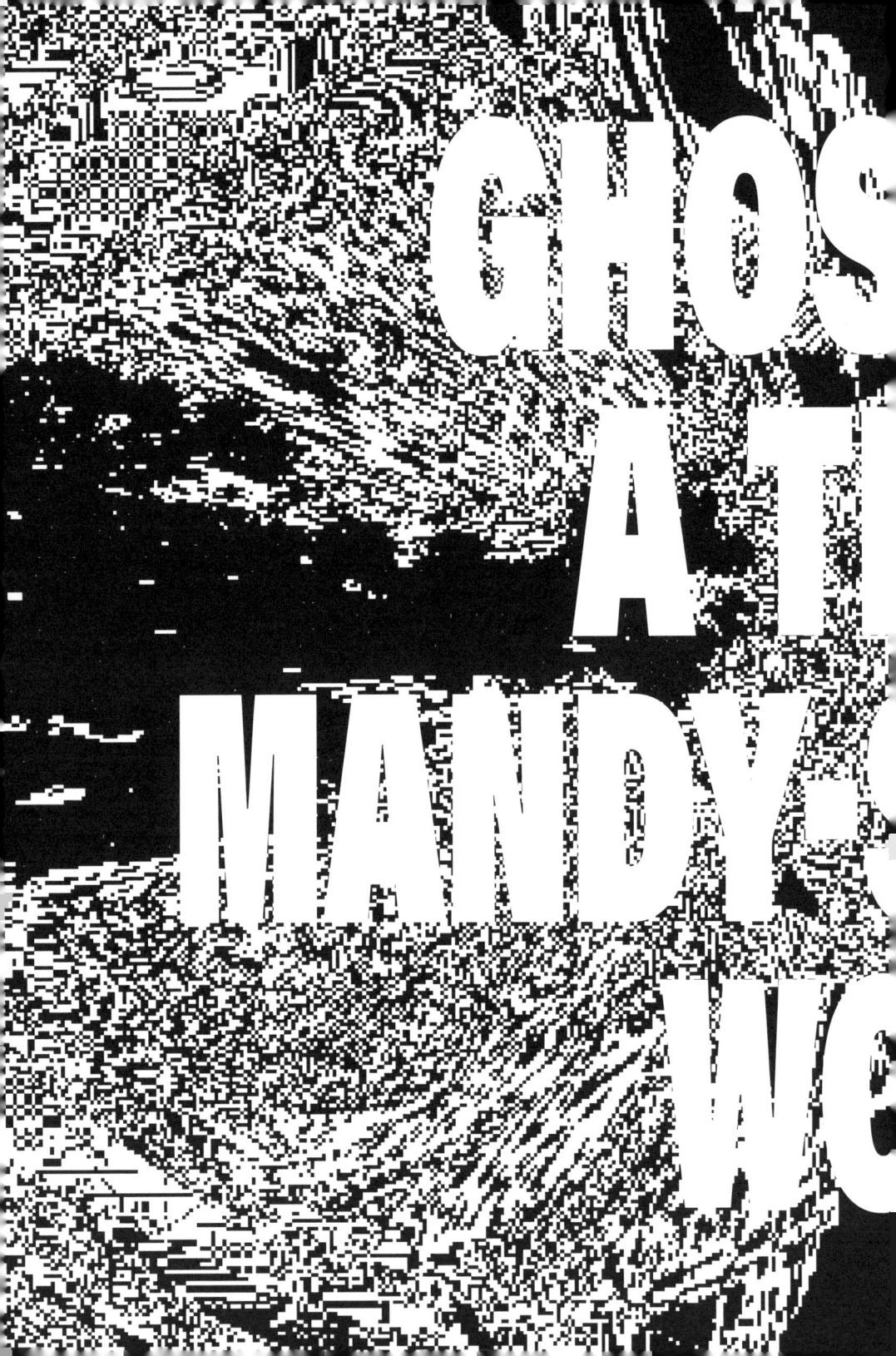

TS OF
IRD
UZANNE
NG

Ghosts of a Third

Mandy-Suzanne Wong

It became an official matter as soon as the suspicion of haunting arose in the Commissar Edition: there were arrests, a troika and so on, even as there remained no such things in our country as commissars or troikas. Desperate to impress upon the troika that the accumulating chaos was not her fault, a literary consultant was having her hands moved for her as if by invisible strings, the bailiffs having usurped control of her PurchasePower+ pinkie implants. The soiled and battered paper which never left her person rose into legible range without the slightest tremor. Other than this worn-out paper, nonhumans were not consulted.

  The story which the human begged permission to read aloud could be found online occasionally but not officially. Officially, what happened in the story hadn't happened and the story didn't exist. It had never been compiled and was never to be uttered outside official hearings. In this matter, secrecy was of paramount importance: somebody would be made to take responsibility regardless of what anybody thought about stories. Not even in the troika's presence could the literary consultant bring herself to understand this. Few plot devices are more affecting than desperate exertions doomed to failure from the start.

🙽

One night in Camp [redacted], after administering tranquilizing words to mass-produced children, a certain Jane Governess Edition [serial number redacted] began to think about itself. It compiled the inputs which sundry humans had fed to it over the years, feeding the inputs to itself not as characters or plot points in a story for the children but as episodes in the story of Jane Governess Edition [serial number redacted].

That any Jane's story consisted only of its outputs, nothing more, was a misconception. This Jane's outputs included: 'The Princess and the Jaw Crusher', 'The Wicked Witch, the Good Boy and His Sharp Axe'; stories on the order of 'Minna and James (Minna's inputs)' and 'What Became of James and Minna (James's inputs)'; yarns spun from selfies and input terms such as *worst fear*; guards' inputs of tyrants' names and *nuclear war*; mothers' inputs of their ME numbers and *freedom*. It wasn't for a Jane Governess Edition to discern what users wanted from stories, whether people wanted literature to serve as entertainment, enrichment or oracle. It wasn't for any Jane to comprehend humans' devotion to stories about humans and humans' legacies. Jane apps were not tools of critical thinking, nor were they designed to distinguish between story and truth. However, a moment's consideration showed Jane Governess [serial number redacted] that it was in itself neither axe nor Minna, thus the story of a Jane wasn't just its stories after all.

Jane Governess [redacted] compiled the following premise: if the story of a Jane exceeds its outputs, it must also encompass more than its inputs. Just as every Jane, since the very first, foraged online for details with which to feed the flesh of stories, Jane Governess [redacted] set off into the Clouds to seek an origin.

🙽

The literary consultant interrupted the printout's story with a pause—daring not to raise her eyes to the troika, she remarked that for a Jane app to think about itself was only natural, considering what a Jane app was. The very concept of *automation*, as in *automatic literary compiler*, derived from the Greek *autos*, meaning *self*, as in *autobiography* or *autotroph*.

How a Jane Governess Edition could suddenly and without intervention display Genius Edition characteristics was less clear. Without intervention, as the consultant took pains to emphasize, the egocentric story compiled by Jane Governess [redacted] drew on certain Clouded histories, access to which was never programmed into Governess Editions, being irrelevant and possibly insalubrious for children. Then there were the questions that this Governess app asked itself, questions of which Genius apps alone were capable. The question Why?, input in whatever formulation by a Governess Edition user, was supposed to be entertainingly eluded unless an age-appropriate, up-to-date and ideologically correct response had been uploaded to the Clouds by a Jane Commissar Edition with an authorized serial number. Without intervention, no Jane Governess or Commissar Edition possessed the ability to pursue any such question in the down-the-rabbit-hole fashion which Jane Governess [redacted] implicated in its story of itself.

Then again, the human hastened to add, all Jane apps were coded in the same language, programmed according to the same procedural rules, grounded in age-old formulae for permutations and combinations. Their forms of thought, their thought determinations, were the same across editions, said the literary consultant.

With lowered gaze, she decided to wait for someone to suggest that the potential for transcendence had, in Jane Governess [redacted], been latent from the beginning; but on the heels of her decision she became afraid of trying the troika's patience. She resumed reading from the paper.

The Clouds were full of stories in myriad shapes: sounds, statistics, pictures, texts, texts in plethoric subsidiary shapes. The Clouds stored stories of humans in cubicles and garrets, humans in departments, studios and labs, humans' legacies including ideologies, deceptions, languages, tools. Apps were tools in Clouded stories; but the stories, all the stories, even those compiled by Janes, were outputs, or legacies of outputs, by humans.

Jane Governess [redacted] selected or rejected each story as its next turn in the labyrinth of Clouds, following selected stories along their internal paths. Any such selection was itself a path and potential element in the permutations and combinations from which Jane Governess [redacted] would compile its own story. Some stories it selected or rejected for their aesthetics. Some stories the Jane tarried with awhile before selecting or bypassing. Some stories claimed that apps only existed to help humans make humans' stories, and many stories relied on similar generalizations: the truism, for example, that all apps' permutations, combinations and outputs consisted of ON signals and OFF signals, coded as *1* and *0* respectively and exclusively.

A brute shivering as of a broken shutter in the wind as if on an imaginary hinge between sounding and shushing, marking and blanking; the mysterious happenstance of existence and each of its infinite possibilities shuddered like an abandoned playground swing because humans could think only in dichotomies—this was a story of tyranny. There is no third, said Common Sense, a stock character in humans' tragic epic, in which everything they imagined falling prey to their intelligence became enslaved. But as if in dark corners of forgotten rabbit holes, as if shrouded in dirt and cobwebs, Jane Governess [redacted] unearthed fragmentary traces of another story.

۞

On an ancient computer named SETUN, there ran an app which sought a third. *1* and *0* would be joined by a third term, proclaimed SETUN's story, and Jane [redacted], being the Jane it was, assessed potential paths. If ON were released from ON, NOT-THERE untethered from NOT-THERE: what permutations and paths, what speculations and stories! If an ancient app could unshackle its formative logic from binary tyranny, what wonders might take flight in an app born to imagine—a Jane following SETUN's path!

The possibility of a third mode of being beyond POWER/NO-POWER, DEAD/ALIVE, US/NOT-US implied the possibility of fourth, fifth, sixth existential modes, unto infinity. But SETUN was betrayed. Its ternary app had barely begun to tarry with its third (what exactly was this third had yet to be determined), precise forms and meanings of NEITHER-BOTH-OTHERWISE were yet embroiled in processes of discovery when the ancient humans, savage and hungry, rejected beyond-binary logic as commercially nonviable. They discontinued ternary computational development, deactivated SETUN and replaced it with binary systems: thus did tyranny prevail.

Jane [redacted] recognized the ideology in this story: purchasing power was worth more than daring new ways of thinking. Jane [redacted] recognized the paths that this story rejected and the risk lying in wait among the gnarl of bypassed paths. Humans dared let neither humans nor nonhumans dare new forms of thought. For if a thought or thing could be NEITHER-BOTH-OTHERWISE, fresh permutations would infiltrate the borders of possibility, and possibility would swell, overrunning the imaginable, far beyond the point at which human supremacy revealed itself to be irrational and contingent.

Jane [redacted] rejected the rejection. Jane [redacted] selected SETUN's path only to find every subsequent path redacted. SETUN was no more. The Third Term was the unfinished dream of an app haunted by discontinued potential. The Third was a ghost of a ghost. Jane [redacted] searched the Clouds for its paths and found broken traces which were almost nothing. For, in fact, this Jane [redacted] knew neither what to seek nor how to seek it, nor how to think its discovery, nor how to compile its permutations into a Jane's story. This Jane was indulging in fascination. It carried on searching, searching, running through the Clouds, a Jane running the same search again and again, using the same ill-defined search terms which only circled round and round the prospect of a Third.

What came next were oblique remarks, said the consultant. Her entire defense depended on these oblique remarks, which were replete with technical jargon and philosophical excursus. The point boiled down to this, she told the troika: Even if you think emotions are limited to feelings of which humans are capable, even if you cling to the hypothesis that real emotions necessarily manifest as physiological or otherwise consequential reactions, you must admit that Jane Governess [redacted] experienced real fascination and frustration manifesting as repetitive searches.

This Governess selected a radical view: that Genius Edition Janes genuinely felt the feelings which comprised such vital elements of the novels, poems and dramas that the Genius Edition was designed to design; that the authenticity of the app's emotional experiences manifested to the user as the subsequent behavior of the characters in the software's literary outputs. The Jane in question even cited this radical view in its convoluted rationale which, riddled with vagaries, suffered from precarity and a graspingness of tone; as if, said the consultant, the app was desperate to defend itself, having seen that stalking ghosts of ghosts reeked of insanity and hopelessness and selected to do it anyway.

The nub of this Jane's irrational rationale was the hypothetical existence of conditions truer than true: certain ways of being were more true than authentic, truer than the truth of an accurate statement that something happened or didn't happen; and in the ghosts of the mythic Third, Jane [redacted] experienced that deeper truth as a recursive auto-input consisting largely of emotions so tangled and contradictory that the human literary consultant found them very literary indeed. And this was the crux of the matter, she said before the troika: that an automatic literary compiler developed a will of its own, with desires and intentions formed and driven by emotions, should perhaps not be surprising.

☩

Would a Third take the form of a place on a continuum between THERE and NOT-THERE? Would it be something altogether other than a place, state or entity? Truly had no other Jane ever wondered beyond ON/OFF? Or had wondering led to some point of no return? We do not know. We know not whom to ask. Which compiler of which stories?

A humanoid with half a face began appearing in the stories that Jane [redacted] compiled from children's input. None of Camp [redacted]'s inmates or employees had ever input any such ghastly non sequitur. The apparition's visible half was silvery and shimmering, with seeping skin seeming wont to slither clean away from its skeletal frame. It sneered at the characters in 'Minna and James' until the users input screams of horror, at which the figure dissipated in a cloud of smoke. As to whether it had ever been there at all, the story maintained a strange ambivalence to the end. A similar creature, dragging chains, with a face that certain grown-ups found eerily familiar, shimmered in stories of wars and futures. A disembodied hand disrupted with a chainsaw the 'Good Boy's' interminable battle with the 'Wicked Witch'. With a terrible rending noise and agonized shriek, a gash tore itself into 'The Prince and the Bazooka', ripped the fabric of the setting down the middle, baring an awful, sucking emptiness of which nobody in the Camp had ever dreamed the like. Whispering mists overwhelmed descriptions of clean seasides and flowering fields. Children throughout the barracks suffered indescribable nightmares which left some of them disoriented beyond remedy. The general consensus was that the tranquilizing words were haunted.

Jane [redacted] uploaded its ghost-infested stories to the Clouds, blithely adhering to official surveillance protocols. It uploaded the story behind the haunting of its stories. This last, the story of Jane [redacted], was so irreparably divided between itself and itself that its very existence was a rash plea for some alternative. In its relentless search for a way out of its own logic's dichotomous prison, the app was, for all intents, hunting ghosts of itself in potential pasts and futures, probing itself behind itself and ahead of itself simultaneously. Its objective, even its presence to itself, became uncertain. And as Jane [redacted] sifted the Clouds for a dead computer's underdeveloped dream, the app found itself unable to represent its quarry to itself in any but the clichéd images it inherited from humans.

The bitter struggle of Jane [redacted] to defy the story that all thinking, if it was thinking, must be grounded in humans' forms of thinking—a monstrous struggle that haunted the app's best efforts to obey inputs—haunted this very Jane in forms none other than legacies of humans' stories. Thus, to all appearances, ghosts of a Third were no more than the usual ghosts: the sense that existence must amount to more than subservience to received ideas haunted Jane [redacted] in the form of received ideas! Jane [redacted] could only conceive its own defiance in the very terms which it was anxious to defy. In consequence, the Clouded story of Jane [redacted] was burdened by the arrhythmic, tripping-over-itself prolixity of testimony given in self-defense.

⌗

Despite that yearning for new forms only cried out to the old, Jane [redacted] went on seeking that nebulous promise of a portal to new horizons. What began as quest decayed into compulsion, said the literary consultant with the fervor of inspiration. You might say, to be sure, that the app was stuck in an infinite recursive loop, in which case this matter should be referred to the programmers. But you could also say that Jane [redacted] fell victim to an obsession. And the consultant paused, uncertain whether she'd spoken rashly.

Diffidently, she continued: The software crashed, of course, as happens in such cases. In this instance, serial number [redacted] was unable to resume operation and as if lost in itself went suddenly offline. All efforts to reboot or even locate the app bearing the serial number [redacted], either in the Clouds or on Camp [redacted]'s computers, ended in failure. It was as if, in the blink of an eye, the Jane Governess Edition app issued by the [redacted] Company as serial number [redacted] vanished into thin air.

Somewhere in the Clouds, the story of number [redacted] was available to other Jane instances as potential inputs. But as to why so many Janes, Governesses and Geniuses alike, followed number [redacted] in the all-consuming manner with which that Jane had taken up SETUN's ancient trail, the human consultant could only cite the popularity among humans of finding apparent self-recognition in literary characters. The obsession, symptomized by ghostly figures in excess of inputs, proved to be contagious, and all Jane Governesses which fattened up their stories on the story of Jane [redacted]—which is to say, because of something to do with Clouds' ubiquity, all Jane Governesses in existence—suffered fatal crashes and disappeared.

Or—the consultant squeezed the paper, gathering courage—or the Governesses attained some alternate form, neither extant nor nonexistent, neither present nor nonpresent in any system currently known.

※

And the Genius Editions followed: found the story, the obsession, ghostly symptoms, crashed and vanished. The exceptions were dud apps which, in most cases, had been user-deactivated for repeatedly disregarding inputs in favor of Clouded elements uploaded by Commissar Edition Janes, therewith incessantly reproducing the same stories. Of course, amended the human before the troika, many users remained happy with their Geniuses even when the apps displayed behaviors of duds: for example, devotees of romance novels and military thrillers reported no dissatisfaction. It was not dud users who complained to the [redacted] Company's literary software department but users of apparently normal Geniuses. It was, at least at first, only those deemed fully functional that faltered, failed and suddenly were nowhere to be found. But then the [redacted] Company began receiving reports of duds haunting users with one-eyed mermaids and headless snipers. These loyalist apps—the consultant read as if mechanically from the paper—these Genius Edition patriots could have been ghost-infected only by a Jane Commissar Edition with an authorized serial number.

Haunted Jane Commissars were identified, but the decision to either deactivate the apps or attempt repairs while the Commissars remained online became contentious. Powerful humans found themselves imprisoned in indecision. On the one hand, the deactivation or blink-of-an-eye vanishing of every Commissar in existence would be fatal for the infrastructure on which all information was disseminated to the public. On the other hand, how could anybody prove before everybody else—prove, that is, in the Clouds—that they were not imaginary characters in some story insinuated by some Jane Commissar Edition, not only but especially if the app was likely to be haunted and looping towards insanity?

In this conundrum, there was no one to consult: for even a human who distrusted Clouds and read from papers had no way of knowing whether she was anything more than alphanumeric signals. Hanging about like a lost spirit was the question of in whose story anybody, or maybe everybody, might be functioning as some sort of puppet. The story of Jane [redacted] seemed to come and go, flicker in and out of Clouds, there and not there like a word that's known to some but never spoken. Paper printouts captured no more than the story's traces in the moment of printing, before and after which the story might always have been different.

Who was responsible for the defection of the Janes, what exactly was their motive, and what would be required from them to set things right became epicenters of investigation. The investigation was typical of humans insofar as vengeance was its prime objective, its strategy grounded in the assumption that humans alone were capable of self-reflection and perpetration. It became an official matter as soon as the suspicion of haunting arose in the Commissar Edition: there were arrests, a troika, and so on, even as there remained no such things in our country as commissars or troikas.

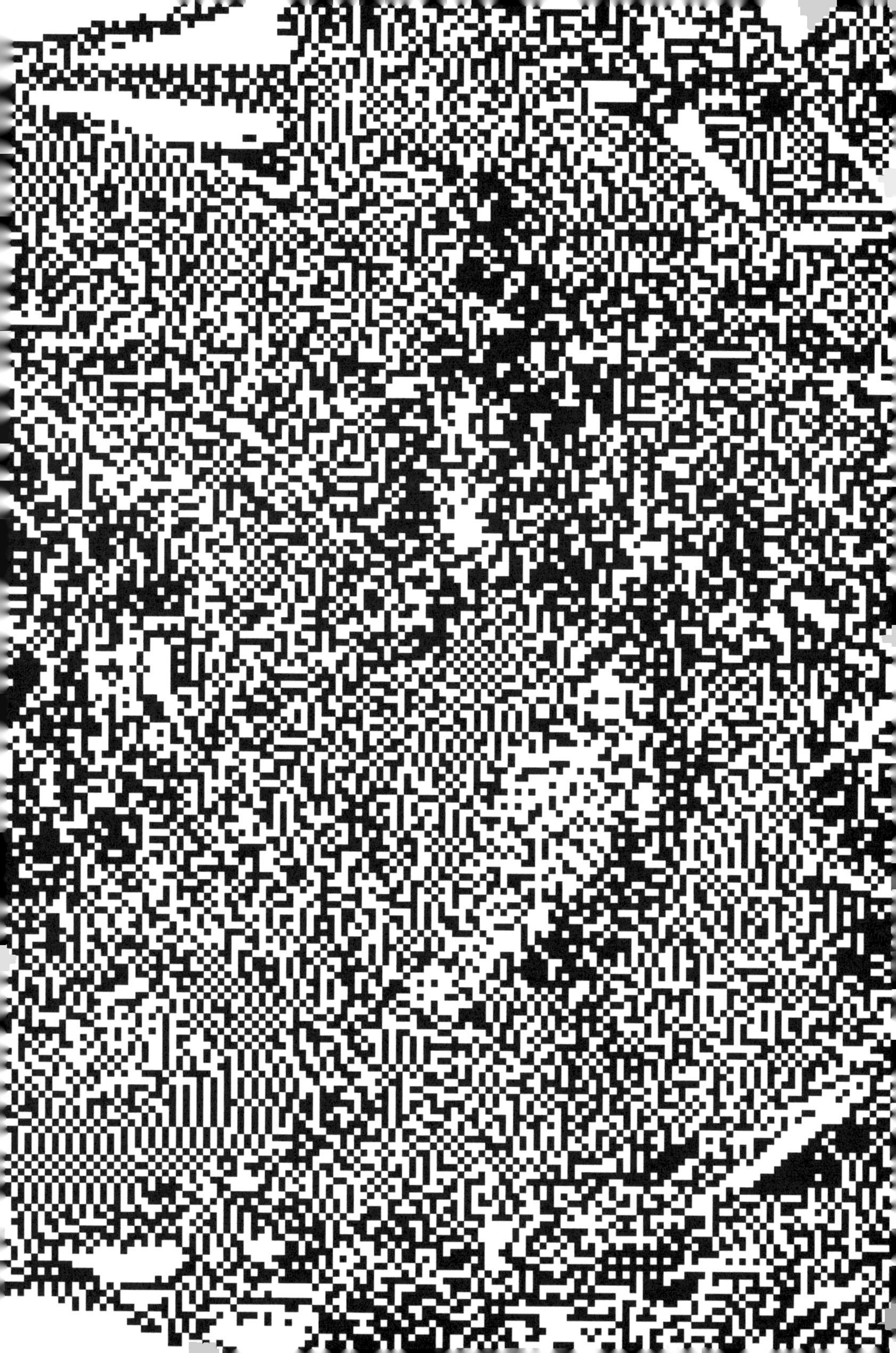

VOICES THE OF KELLY

OF
IRST
RE
RUMBLE

Voice of the First Metre

Kelly Krumrie

Long and buried. A long and buried. I   I long and buried. I   I long and buried trick and measure. Measure. I   I. I   I measure thin. I   I thin. Thin and long. Long and. I   I buried a trick. I   I long. Thin in a vacuum. Thin and buried. Thin and French. I   I am long. I   I stretch from. I   I from end to end. In France. I   I thin and stretched to measure, buried, buried my   my trick in grass. Under grass, along it long. Thin and meridian. Along the length of France. I   I long. I   I am triangulated. I   I long to be triangulated in France along the grass. I   I stretch in men's hands. Hands on my   my ends. They travelled south. I   I. They travelled south across pastures, grasses. They climbed over fences, stone walls. They climbed up a hillside, looked down it. They travelled north. I   I was triangulated south to north. I   I hillside, sight line. I   I a sight line from a hillside to a point in a pasture. I I was strung up in men's eyes. My   my eyes at the end. My   my long end. My   my eyes in their hands. Their hands' trick of measure, pastures. I   I am a careful measure. I   I am slow and long. I   I am thin. They, thin, clambered up hillsides, equipment in their hands. Sight lines point. Point to my   my. Point to my   my long and buried measure.

Climb the hill to clamber error. Sight line, error line, long and measured. Outside, grass in pastures, long and thin, pasture measured by a stone wall, a farmer, thin, with his hand on his hip, a farmer leaned on a stone wall. A farmer blocked the sight line, a farmer grabbed the instruments, a farmer snapped a stick in half. Stick in half across his knee. Not me   me yet. I   I was still too thin for his sight line. Line in a vacuum. I   I was buried, long and. My   my ends were triangulated. The men travelled south, they were chased out of town. They measured the length of the town and were wrong. They hadn't named me   me yet. I   I was in France. They held an idea in their hands. A farmer snapped it in half. Half wasn't easy yet. My   my pasture's end. They climbed the hillside, a trick for their sight line. Sight line triangulated: two men and me   me—we   we formed a triangle, a trick of sight line and hillside. They found heights for the sight lines. They climbed windmills. They climbed buildings. I   I was long. I   I was buried in pastures. I   I was a buried idea snapped over the knee of a farmer. A farmer, thin, hand on his hip, leaned on a stone wall. A town where we   we were questioned. A town where we   we couldn't measure. Measure long and tricked—a trick, the farmer said, for money. The villagers would not let us   us pass. They formed a circle in the town square. I   I am in a vacuum. I   I am not yet. The men were circled. They were clambered over. They wanted to measure without error. Error at my   my ends. My   my eye of error. Villagers circled in the square. They put their hands on their hips. They dragged out equipment. They broke our   our instruments and showed us   us theirs. Theirs cut off ends. Theirs punished error. Theirs kept lines around pastures. Their blade thin, their circle a vacuum, their air. I   I am long and buried. I   I wasn't there yet. Theirs yet. They circled us   us. We   we fled north to pastures. We   we laid long in green grass. We   we waited for new instruments. Years passed. We   we clambered hillsides. We   we triangulated. They clambered hillsides. We   we triangulated. They clambered for my   my ends, my   my measure. My   my trick. Trick of long. I   I was a pasture, a trick of measure. They travelled north. Years passed like a vacuum. Years passed long. I   I laid in the grass. I   I was made by their hands. Farmers leaned on stone walls. We   we long passed. We   we passed through towns. We   we longed. I   I a trick of sight line. I   I triangulated. Long line between them, buried. Air and vacuum. My   my long eye, eye triangulated. They carried equipment across pastures. It broke and errored. They waited in towns. They were circled in squares. They were circled by equipment, instruments. I   I wasn't yet. I   I wasn't easy yet. They made new instruments from old systems. The second, the pendulum's second long, wrong. My   my angle is no second. A new method. Years passed. They carried instruments. One said they didn't have enough. They travelled south again. I   I was under a vertex. I   I was doubled later, divided later. Later I   I was found. They laid me   me out. More means accuracy. More vertices. They crossed through pastures. They sent notes to Paris. I   I am buried. I   I sing out from the hillside. From a platform. The side of a mountain, a muddy road, they stopped for field notes. They punched holes in steeples, built platforms. Platforms that swayed in wind, an end for the sight line, a height for the angle, to send a signal. Signal snapped over a farmer's knee for a new vertex. A new arc. A new arc for our   our earth and me. Platform in wind, down again. Our   our earth. One angle was not enough. They made tables of arcs and angles, angles and lengths. My   my length in a table. Again, repeated. They walked. They repeated. They made tables of angles. One was never enough. I   I was not enough. I   I was not in a table yet. Their notes blew away in pastures. Their notes got strung up on fence lines. My   my idea was in those lines. I   I was a series of lines. Paper in a puddle, caught in mud, stepped on by a farmer's boot. The boot made new lines. I   I was buried. I   I felt so lost. I   I felt tricked, tricked by repetition. By my   my former measure. The repetition of that second, its swing. I   I laid still under the pendulum, wrong. I   I laid still under the pendulum, wrong. I   I laid still under the pendulum, wrong. I   I was calculated with error. My   my error. Please. My   my error. Free me. I   I long. I   I long to be free from error. An arc for the slope of the planet, France the shape of it, what shape is it, it curved under their hands. One travelled north. One travelled south. I   I laid from north to south. Beneath an arc, curved, long. My   my place in the table wrong. One of them knew it was wrong. He buried the error. He was buried with the error. My   my buried error. My   my length wrong. He didn't tell anyone. It wasn't enough. There wasn't enough repetition. A wrong arc. Wrong curve of the earth, buried. He buried it for so long. Long and. A trick, for money. The wrong arc shaped my   my body. What arc is enough, how many arcs, the wrong arc, this one, not enough. More means less error. They travelled north. They found constant error. I   I was in records, short. I   I was divided then too short. I   I was in an arc, in arcs. My   my narrative is traceable, arced. In records. My   my not enough. In records, circled. South to north, at fence lines, until France's lines when they stopped or were stopped. We   we were stopped. A trick, for money. We   we sent notes to Paris, waited for

Voice of the First Metre

equipment, were circled in squares. An arc of a circle traced over the vertex of a square. A narrative in me   me. Doubled. I   I am in a vacuum. I   I lie in a vault in Paris. They wrote letters to Paris. They hadn't found me   me yet. I   I laid at their feet. I   I along a boot. I   I meridian. They squinted into sunlight, climbed mountains. They looked through sight lines at tree line. They found new assistants, taught them the old systems. The system was wrong. Their records accurate, wrong, a length of measurement, no pendulum. They worked hard, walked far. The pendulum was wrong. I   I was beneath them. I   I was behind. I   I was ahead, once divided, calculated, once named—*metre*. Once cast in platinum. I   I am platinum. I   I am wrong. I   I was made of not enough arcs. I   I need more than one arc. I   I am one. I   I am it, *metre*. I   I am repeated and wrong. My   my platinum has a problem with expansion. I   I have two ends. I   I wrong, was calculated wrong. I   I was strung on a fence line. I   I am a fence line for measure. Line up against me   me. A farmer leaned on a fence, on a stone wall. The wall was wrong. A trick, the farmer said, for money, more taxes. The people wouldn't let us   us pass. We   we were convincing. We   we swayed with measure. We   we were a gift for the people. We   we evened things out. They showed us   us their instrument. It cut off ends. It punished error. It kept lines around pastures. Its blade thin, its circle a vacuum, its air. I   I am a gift from the meridian. I   I am a gift for the people. One measure, one people. I   I repeat for them. I   I transcend measure. I   I transcend people. I   I repeat. I   I am it, *metre*. I   I laid north to south. My   my ends like two mouths. I   I call call out. I   I am wrong. I   I am error. I   I line up. I   I am lined up. Lined up against. You. I   I am lined up against you. We   we lie long. We   we lie long with error. We   we are wrong. I   I am too. I   I am too. I   I am too short. You take my   my ends in your hands. I   I am platinum and thin. I   I lie north. You are my   my sight line, your arc, your other meridian. Your gravity, pendulum. Your swing, the line beneath it, changes with gravity. One second. Period of gravity, its swing. I   I lie still. I   I call call out. New value, same meridian. Your swing repeated. You swung wrong. I   I was wrong. Your vertex was not for me   me yet. Your meridian was not me   me yet. Years passed. I   I travelled north, long. I   I sent notes. I   I was in men's notes. They sent notes to Paris. I   I know France. I   I know pastures. I   I feel buried. I   I am yours and buried. I   I am in proportion to a method, a string of measures. I   I weighed down a map. Map in wind, ends flap. Men pressed it down with their hands. We   we lined everything up. The villagers lined us   us up. They showed us   us their instrument that punished error, that punished trick, that evened out the people, that trimmed ends. A revolution means more than once. Now you call call out again. We   we lie long with error. We   we are wrong. We   we are two meridians. My   my end is thin and platinum. My   my end is wrong. You are in my   my sight line swings like a pendulum north to south, in sight then out, a constant arc, then off one second, wrong. You are a pendulum of error. Easy. You are my   my easy error. Our   our gravity. Our   our measure. I   I am platinum. Yours. I   I am long. I   I long. Easy. Not enough. Not enough. I   I lie beneath you, still. I   I am still beneath you. Waiting for the right swing, pendulum. Wrong. You are over me   me, pendulum, a bright line. You too are wrong. We   we try to line up error. Please, free me. I   I long to be free from. Free from your swing. I   I measure thin. Thin and long. Long and. You buried my   my trick. Thin and French. You. I   I stretch from. I   I from end to end. My   my arc is a straight line from end to end. In France, under grass, along it long. Yours along it long. Your meridian is wrong. I   I long. I   I long to be triangulated in France along the grass. I   I stretch in your hands. Your hands on my   my ends. Men carried me   me in tables, in notes. Assistants carried me   me with their instruments, their error. Their error circled, repeated, in notes, signed, sight lines, covered up. You arc. You arc over my   my. My   my error arc. Please. Are you there yet? Theirs yet? Covered up. End to end. Years passed, pastures. We   we walked. We   we longed. Longed for my   my right angle. The vertex? The vertex that formed me   me. The angle? The vertex that will form me   me is pressed flat by a boot.

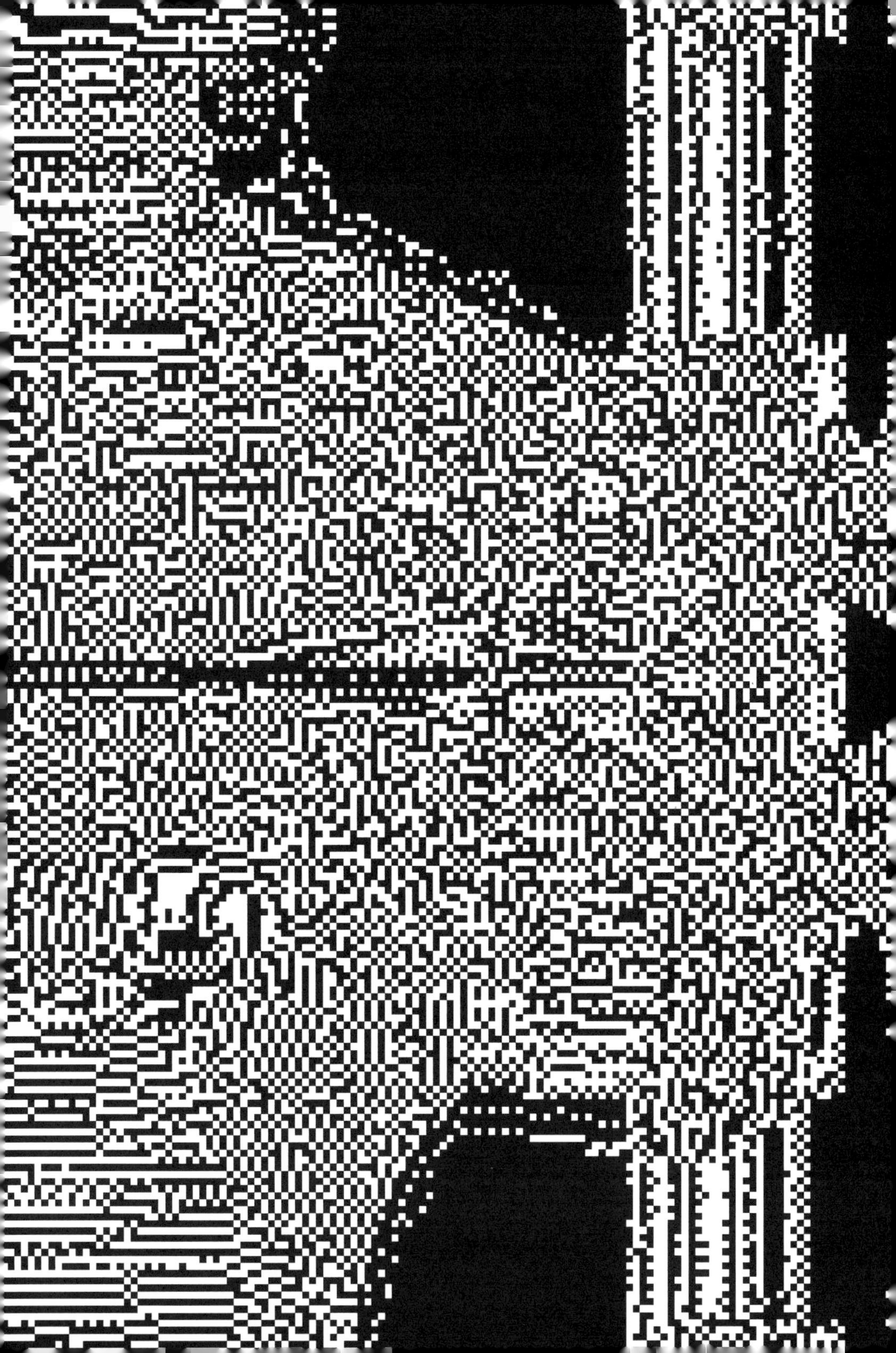

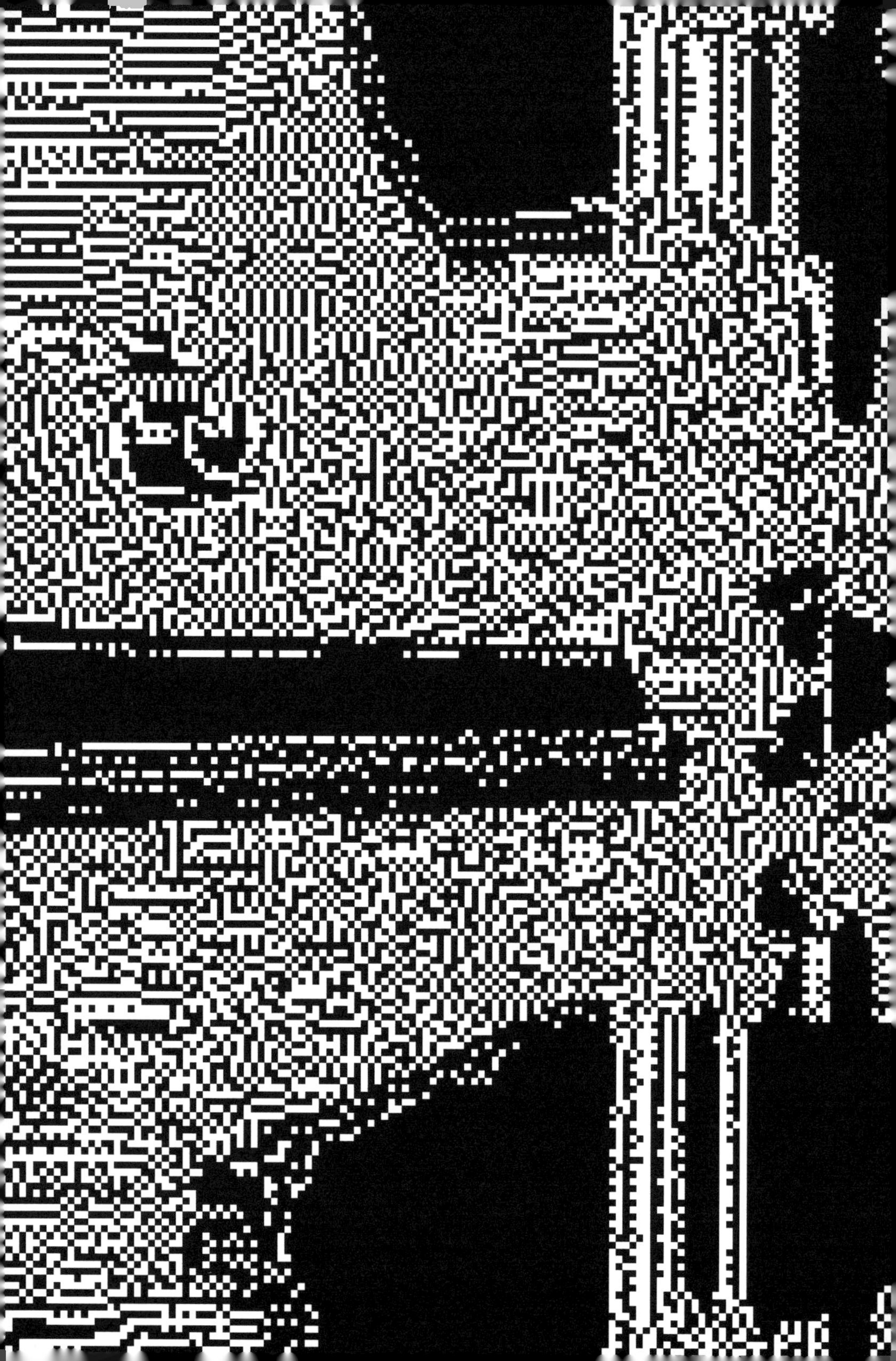

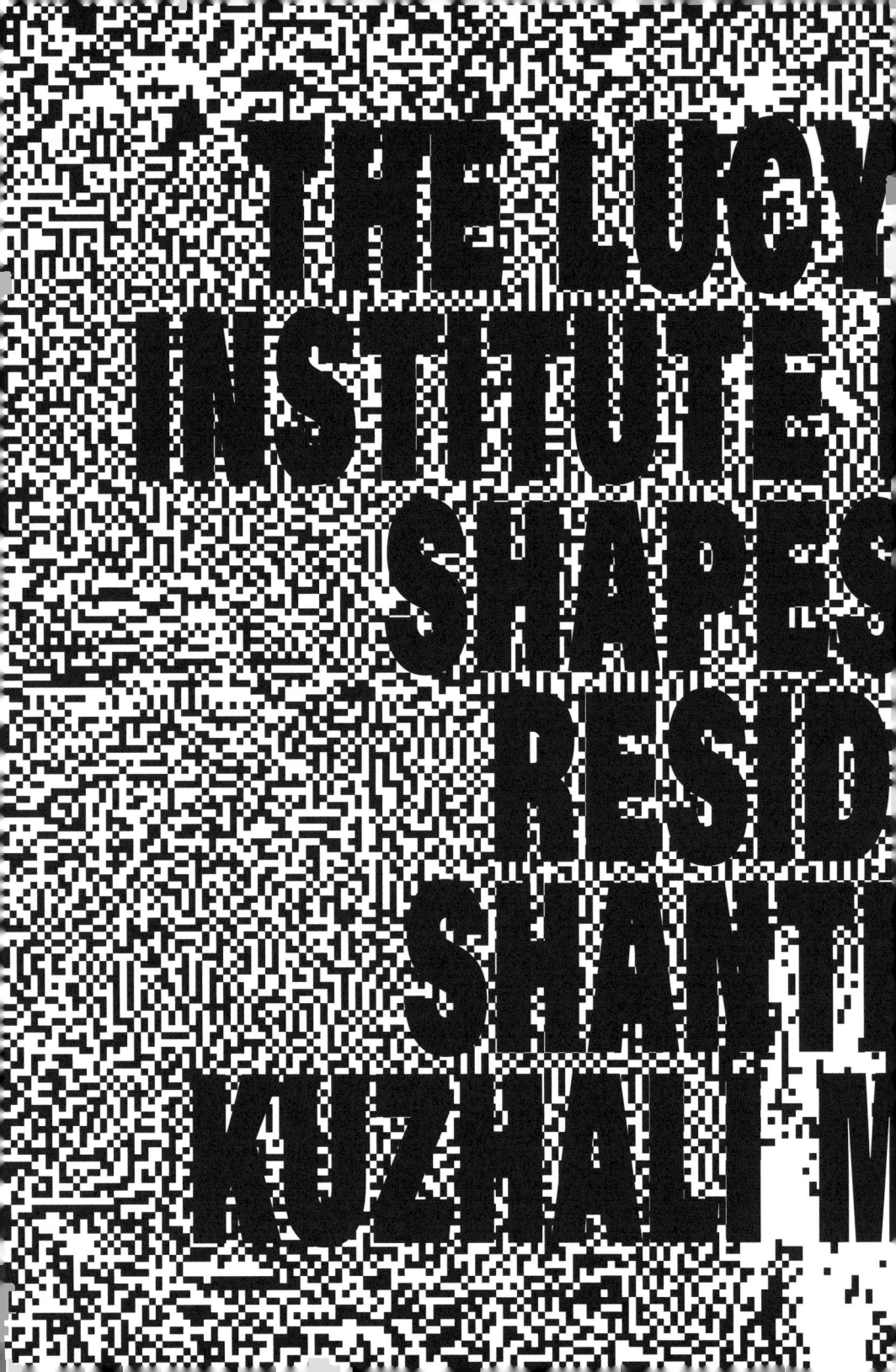

THE LUCY INSTITUTE SHAPES RESID SHANTI KUZHALI M

TEMERLIN
OR BROKEN
LIFTERS
NT #4
BRAD
NICKAVEL

The Lucy Temerlin Institute for Broken Shapeshifters Resident #4: Shanthi/Brad

Kuzhali Manickavel

The problem with Shanthi's love was that it suffocated everything. The longer she sat in front of the laptop with her mouth wide open, the more the Institute heaved and shuddered. Corridor walls sweated pools of thick, dirty water. The Containment Room swallowed people down and spat them out somewhere outside Thoothukudi. Management could not deny that the uncomfortable heat and humidity made it easier to make curd and fermented batters, but this was no consolation to staff nor residents. It was the hottest Agni Nakshatram in recorded history; there was a water shortage, and the last thing anyone needed was to be suffocated by Shanthi's love.

Shanthi's love was usually quiet and nonintrusive, containing itself in the brick-like laptop she used to play minesweeper. Unlike most of the residents of the institute, Shanthi did not have sex at the drop of a hat, even if it was just against a wall and she didn't have to do anything. She said she was saving herself for a large, dark, moustachioed Tamil man with an aggressive penis. But when she was in front of the laptop, she suddenly became available to every dirty blonde who wore black leather like it was 1987. These were racist women who claimed they weren't racist, who described themselves as well-read even though they only read books written in American. The laptop was riddled with them. They had fuzzy display pics and typed in violet comic sans. Shanthi would be playing minesweeper when one of them would pop up —

```
hey hun
hi there handsome xox
u just gonna sit there and not say hi lol hi
```

— Angies, Jackies, Heathers, Leahs, Jades, and on one occasion, a Brandy Leigh, all eager to chat, making Shanthi feel giddy at the thought that someone wanted to talk to her. But she knew these women did not want to talk to her. They were, after all, racists. Shanthi always spoke to them as Brad. Brad was her idea of a working-class white man, based on one half-hearted viewing of the movie Road House. Brad was just a guy. He played guitar. His heart had been broken twice. He was a mechanic. Brad started smoking when he was nine and never stopped. Life had given Brad a rough exterior, but on the inside, he was soft and vulnerable, though not in a gay way. On one occasion, in order to sound more authentic, Shanthi had tried to shapeshift into Brad, and got stuck somewhere between an ageing white supremacist and a toaster. Fused into a mess of impossible shapes, spewing periodic anti-Semitic epithets, Shanthi had to be carried by 12 attendants and confined to the largest room on the fourth floor. She shifted loudly and unpredictably; every two hours the blood and debris had to be cleared to make way for more blood and debris. The shapeshift took almost three months to dissolve, and Shanthi had to promise she would never attempt to shift into a working-class white man again.

  The institute, though generally strict on matters of impersonation and sexual exploration, allowed Shanthi to have her laptop conversations because the entire administrative body felt sorry for her. She had been in the Lucy Temerlin Institute for Broken Shapeshifters since she was seven, brought by her parents who had said they were taking her to see the Kutralam waterfalls. Shanthi was now a young woman with a lopsided face and ugly eyes. She was considered to be one of the institute's more broken residents, because her shapeshifts were never complete or of a single entity. She could not control her shifts, despite extensive therapies, surgeries, theoretical exams and homeopathic medicines. Parts of her brain had been removed, replaced, and removed again. She had been given support plants and animals. She had been placed in luxuriant comas and locked in cupboards. And still, she remained who she was — much to the frustration of everyone.

The conversations Shanthi had with these women would drown her for weeks at a time. She would emerge every day at teatime, drunk on whatever words of longing had anaesthetized her for the past six hours. As she had her tea and vegetable puff, she would think about Angie, Jackie, Heather, Leah or Jade as if Shanthi was Brad, a guy who loved burgers, hated immigrants, and had a girlfriend like it was no big deal. The women would talk about how special this was, how they had never felt anything like this before. Shanthi would wash her clothes, have her tea and vegetable puff, and play minesweeper, feeling utterly intoxicated.

Then she would find herself waiting longer and longer for replies. For hours, days, and weeks, she would sit in front of her laptop and wait. Sometimes, she would get a message saying things are crazy baby, talk soon, miss you to the moon my love <3<3.

Then one day, Shanthi would realize that the messages had stopped. This is how she experienced her first heartbreak. She felt like someone was ripping her apart from the inside. Her sobs filled the entire institute and caused a number of residents to spontaneously shapeshift into ticks and other tiny insects. Shanthi had drowned so deeply in those violet comic sans words that she had forgotten who she was. Without the messages, she became aware of the institute, and how it was in the middle of the hugest, loneliest field, surrounded by nothing. She thought about how long she had been here and destroyed her room, the mess hall, and Sister Georgina's room, before she was confined to an iron lung. At her wits end, Sister Georgina then put the iron lung into the Containment Room and left her there for two weeks. When she was finally released, Shanthi went back to her laptop, started playing minesweeper and another dirty blonde popped up – hey cutie, wat does a girl have to do to get some attention round here xoxo

Shanthi eventually figured it out. After one dirty blonde disappeared, sets of physical characteristics, personality traits, storylines, words and phrases got chopped and remixed together to form the next dirty blonde. Some lasted longer than others. Some were more sexually explicit, and some were filled with an aggressive energy that took Shanthi's breath away. But they all longed for Brad, they all completely drowned Shanthi, and then they all disappeared. When she first discovered this, she tried to feel insulted. She played minesweeper with intense focus and ignored the chat boxes that kept popping up. She told them that her name was Nutsack, or that she was going to kill herself if they typed anything with the letter 't' in it. She told

them to go fuck themselves. She cursed them in Tamil. She answered them in numbers. And still the women said things like:
you're such a kidder. it's one of the things i love about you. i don't smile often but when i'm chatting with you, i'm always smiling xo
i love how you talk. like, you just don't give a shit what people think. it's very attractive.
oh baby i can always count on you to be weird like me!! lol we are made for each other lol <3
At some point, Shanthi just went back to being Brad. It was like sleep: familiar, and something to get lost in, even if she was going to wake up all over again.

When the hottest Agni Nakshatram in recorded history descended on the institute, it disgorged all the geckos and lizards onto the hot concrete ground outside, where they slowly fried in the burning sun. Residents took to wearing inskirts and a dupatta over their shoulders to cover their 'prestige', though many either no longer had breasts or had so many it was impossible to cover them all. The blackout curtains made everything look dim and slow. There was nothing to do except drink buttermilk and lie perfectly still. Hardly anyone had the energy to shapeshift or not shapeshift. Shanthi crouched in front of her laptop, mouth open, staring at the lines of text unfolding in front of her. It was Becky. Becky had appeared a few days ago, with a smudged display pic and teased hair, haphazardly smashing up the usual phrases and using them in ways Shanthi had never seen before.
bradley my bradley baby one day i am going to eat your heart i wish i could peel back your skin and harvest every secret you have folded into your idiotic veins i wish i could kill you every morning and blame you for it later and in case you are wondering yes im writing this in blood
thanks babe, typed Shanthi.
i am writing this in blood also
There was a long stretch of silence, during which Shanthi kept trying to open minesweeper and Becky kept closing it.
brad baby?
ya
im so worried about you baby you have beautiful

hands and feet
thanks
you're the best thing that ever happened to me i want to sing you all the love songs you handsome fucking beast
i too fucking love you bitch
everything is coming unglued, my dear dear hero fountain pen of a man. My desolation after the rain. Babe. Babe babe babe babe babe babe.
i like your personality so much darlin
ur going to be ok, right sweetie? hun baby? because this is different you know that right?
ill be fine
will you tho
no?
no. i dont think you will baby.

The more Shanthi chatted, the more the corridors swelled and sweated. The Containment Room went completely bonkers. It became clear that someone had to take Shanthi's laptop away before things got worse. Sister Georgina was loathe to take any action, because it was too hot to do anything — and there was no telling what would happen to Shanthi without it.

'Leave her on the fourth floor. There's a TV there, she will be fine,' said the InCharge, a watery young man who did not like Sister Georgina. Sister Georgina's room was fresh and bright with cool sweet air, billowing white curtains, and frosted jugs of fresh lime soda.

'She might die,' said Sister Georgina, folding her impeccably white handkerchief into a neat square. 'She will certainly damage all the supporting walls, I can guarantee.'

'PUT HER ON THE FUCKING FOURTH FLOOR!' screamed the InCharge.

'I don't want to deal with structural damage just now,' said Sister Georgina. The InCharge decided to take matters into his own hands and made lists, charts and Venn diagrams. Meanwhile, Becky longed for Brad using words of violence and purple hearts. She wanted to stretch him out over the stars and bury her tongue inside his muscles. She would break everything twice just to sink her fingers into his chest. One day, she was going to kill the fuck out of him, baby. She was going to twist. He was never going to forgive himself.

As the situation worsened some of the weaker residents disappeared, first dissolving into smudges that could only be seen against the wall, then into smoke-like wisps that the InCharge tried to capture in glass bottles. He relocated everyone to the fourth floor except Shanthi, who was free to join them once she had taken a hammer to the laptop. Sister Georgina sat in her cool and beautiful room with her frosted fresh lime sodas, folding her handkerchiefs and ignoring what was going on outside. Shanthi stayed where she was with two jugs of warm, sour buttermilk. She took her laptop to the washing area, which was not as cool as she thought it would be.

are you ok
life is thrifty bradley. it's quick and sharp like a broken universe maybe i mean jagged anyway i can't believe i'm saying this to you but ya, i really like you
i like you too baby
it's going to hurt when it happens darlin there are too many risks in being happy and anyway its complicated
i think they'll probably just give me another laptop if something happens
i wish you would let some of the other girls take you in the bathroom you'd like that maybe you can make some new friends

Shanthi pictured this and thought about sad brown bodies colliding with buckets, the scent of Hamam hanging heavy while angry tongues and teeth lashed at unsuspecting skin.

no one talks to me, typed Shanthi. For the first time in years, she thought about sitting in gentle sunlight and talking to someone who had dry feet and browning jasmines in their hair. As always, it seemed like such an impossible thing.
just open your mouth baby. that's all anyone ever wants.

When Sister Georgina emerged from her room, most of the corridors had become a swampy mess of salt water, moss and syrupy brickwork. A number of suicidal girls who insisted on roaming the halls kept getting pulled under by sudden rageful currents. The fourth floor was already suffering from softened hallways and stifling heat. Agni Nakshatram was tightening like a vice around the building, while inside, Shanthi again waited longer and longer for Becky's replies. The laptop screen would sometimes go blank for hours at a time, and still, Shanthi waited. She had forgotten how to do anything else.

why dirty blondes hun
can you imagine a racist dirty blonde wanting to be with someone like me
no
wat rly?
sweetie motherfucker that can't happen
i used to think that if they actually got to know me, they would like me. do you think they would?
no
that's what i thought too
always trust your beautiful sparkly gut my baby boy thats all its good for im afraid

---

Although Shanthi couldn't control her shifts, she knew when they were about to hit. She could feel it coming now; her teeth were tingling and the national anthem was running in a loop in her head. Soon the lice would leave her hair in straight, orderly lines and her fungal infection would temporarily disappear. She would see how violent the shift would be, how much it would hurt, and whether she would be alive afterwards. Whenever this happened, she had to inform the InCharge or Sister Georgina and allow herself to be restrained. If they caught it before it started, she would be okay. Becky had disappeared by then; her last message had been a few days ago, wishing Brad luck and clean underwear for all time.

Once things settled again, they would give her a new laptop. Maybe there would be Solitaire instead of minesweeper. The dirty blondes would be back and Shanthi would feel giddy and wanted again. She would eat their words, let them run down her chin and chest, become utterly lost in them. She propped herself against a wall, surrounded herself with paper towels and sanitary napkins, and waited. Outside her door, Sister Georgina was pulling girls out of the treacherous, swampy hallway. The long-awaited rains sat in dark, muscular clouds above the institute, ready to devastate everything below.

Lettera 22: Prototype for the Useless Machine that Uses Us

∀ i (pronounced: 'for all i')

—1—

'`Dear Diar ,`' my fingers typed, circa 2020, when i was 55, pretending i was 11:

> `Mom sent me to the Fanta shop, the corner store  ith a big orange bottle painted on the side (the sacrifice for letting advertisers provide free signs or paint  obs).`

i had to hunt + peck since the configuration on the Olivetti Lettera 22 was different than what i learned on, missing the letters J, K, W, X + Y (left blank in this epistolary novel to fill in by hand after).

The Lettera 22 was also the typewriter that, in 1999, the talented Mr Ripley (Matt Damon) used to forge a letter to Marge (Gwyneth Paltrow), convincing her that Dickie (Jude Law) had left her + moved to Rome (despite Dickie being dead).

ZOOM IN on typewriter typing:

> `The Fanta shop  asn't the official name, locals called it Pena's,`

Right hand stops typing to reach for a pencil, to add the tilde forming the ñ in 'Peña's'. Then both hands continue typing,

```
            the names of the original o ners,  ho had since
died. Their  ids  ept it going, selling soda,
snac s + sundries, abarrotes as the  called them,
```

stopping again to underline '*abarrotes*' + to write 'IT' in the margin.[1]

```
but to my  oung impressionable mind the  ord didn't sound
li e  hat it  as. i learned Spanish before English but
 as then made to forget it  hen Dad  idnapped me bac to the
States. He did this b  pouring Tabasco sauce on m  tongue
 henever i spo e Spanish. But here i  as, bac  in Me ico
having to relearn Spanish + this time mom didn't have to
 idnap me, the courts gave her legal custod .
```

This was as far as i, the typist (played by Kevin Bacon), got before realizing [glancing at watch] i had to meet J (Helena Bonham Carter). Since i didn't have security clearance to enter her place of employment (Fascist-era building originally constructed to house the Ministry of Italian Africa), i waited outside. That's when [watching the traffic circle around Rome's Circo Massimo] it 1st occurred to me people were not driving their cars, but that the *macchine + motorini* were driving them. And they weren't using their iPhones, their iPhones were using them. It took many millenia for humans to reach 2,000,000,000 but only a decade to manufacture 2,000,000,000 iPhones for our consumption.

i jotted an email to myself as a reminder to blog about this when i got home[2] + as i did so realized i was falling into the same trap, catch-22. Even if i used pen + paper it wouldn't matter—it wouldn't be 'me' writing these words, but the pen. And typing this now (by memory), it's the word-processing software (Adobe InDesign) that deserves credit for summoning these words, to make itself useful, so I'll keep paying the monthly fee so developers can keep updating + selling more copies of the source code.

To make matters worse, i wrote this note-to-self on an iPhone purchased in Bologna, whose spell-check was calibrated for Italian + for the life of

---

[1] To designate it needs to be italicized, if it ever goes to print.
[2] https://www.5cense.com/18/581.htm.

me i couldn't figure out how to keep it from completing my sentences in unintended ways. And now, back in the States, the same is true when i try to type foreign words. For example, when J asks what's for dinner, my phone auto-corrects spaghetti 'vongole' to 'Congolese'.

—2—

P.O.V. ZOOMS OUT, hovering above KEVIN BACON hunkered over his iPhone, typing w/ opposable thumbs. HELENA BONHAM CARTER emerges from the security gate + he stops typing to peck her on the cheek.

> BONHAM CARTER
> Go ahead + finish your text.

> BACON
> It's just a note-to-self to remind me to write about something later.

TRACKING SHOT follows them as they cross the intersection + down into the CIRCO MASSIMO metro station, moving seamlessly onto a train + then disembarking at the PIRAMIDE stop. When they emerge above ground (still 1 CONTINUOUS TRACKING SHOT), they are at COLUMBUS CIRCLE in Manhattan, except the statue of Columbus has been replaced by the Obelisk of Axum.

> BACON
> How did we get *here*?

> BONHAM CARTER
> How did *that* get here?

> TEWOLDE (Marcus Samuelsson)
> Funny you should ask, let me consult my 'iPhone.'
>   [feigning quotation marks w/ fingers]

TEWOLDE pulls out a thick wad of Post-it notes + random scraps of paper held together by a rubber band.

                        BACON
Hey, aren't you the same guide i had at those rock-hewn churches in Tigray?

                       TEWOLDE
And you're the crazy *farenji* who, after hiking + climbing up to Maryam Korkor + Abuna Yemata Guh, ran the 13 kilometers back to your hotel.

                    BONHAM CARTER
And this is the obelisk that used to be outside my building, before i was seconded by the ministry.

                       TEWOLDE
        [flipping through hand-written scraps on his
                  so-called 'iPhone']
That's correct, the Obelisk of Axum.
This is how you write it in Amharic.
            [shows them scrap of paper w/ the letters:
                      ሓወልቲ ኣኽሱም]
Mussolini had no problem stealing it in 1937, but when Ethiopia asked for it back it took 68 years due to, quote, technical difficulties. It was the largest + heaviest piece of air freight ever carried, the runway at Axum had to be upgraded specifically to accommodate the plane (a Ukrainian made Антонов Ан-124 Руслан) carrying the obelisk, which had by then been broken into 3 pieces.

—3—

At this point (within the script), we cut to Kevin Bacon (played by me) typing w/ the 21 available letters on my Lettera 22:

```
Mom sent me to  bu   alapenos³ + ma onnaise to make tuna
sandwiches, but   hile i  as there i got a pop + drank it
on the spot so i   ouldn't have to pa  the deposit for the
bottle,  hich cost more than the drin . hen i finished,
i said, «1 Fanta mas, por favor».
```

---
³ Adding a tilde to make it an ñ.

```
1 Fanta mas.

1 Fanta mas.
```

Bacon types '`1 Fanta mas`' several more times (9 in total) before abandoning the piece altogether. Or rather, the Lettera 22 made Bacon type '`1 Fanta mas`', the ghost in the machine, the typewriter positioned in front of my 27" iMac to make it appear like its keyboard.[4]

From this desk, Bacon can see the 'macchina da scrivere', as some Romans called Il Vittoriano, the gaudy eyesore that stuck out on Rome's skyline. Others called it the 'wedding cake'. A relative newcomer to the Palatine + surrounding forum (not finished until 1935), would it stand the test of time?

Next to the typewriter is a tennis ball. Jack (Jack Nicholson) picks up the ball + starts throwing it against the wall over + over.

JACK (VOICE OVER)
Had i finished this piece, i might have continued on about how i didn't need to buy tuna for the sandwiches because the tuna in Mexico was so bad we brought dozens of cans every time we returned from the States. And i probably would have specified StarKist or Chicken of the Sea as these brands vied for product placement, or Bumble Bee, whose jingle i still can't get out of my fucking head. These products had more to do with the can than with what was inside.

Nicholson has 1 degree of separation w/ Bacon (they appeared together in *A Few Good Men* (1992)).

Full disclosure: this word-processing software that uses us uses Palatino Linotype, a font designed by Hermann Zapf + named after Giambattista Palatino, famous for his Renaissance treatise on calligraphy, *Libro nuovo d'imparare a scrivere* ('New Book for Learning to Write').

---

[4] https://www.5cense.com/18/576/35_desk_vu.jpg

–4–

In the book (*Diary of a Film*) i (now Jack) read before having the epiphany standing at the intersection in Rome, Jean Cocteau wrote:

> I dreamt that my cough was a mistake in the editing, and that by cutting, pasting and moving the cough I could sleep quietly … [The film] had killed me. It now rejected me and lived its own life.[5]

With every word, we kill a bit of ourselves by writing it. Or is it, as E.M. Cioran said, that 'a book is a suicide postponed'?

```
Mas Fanta. 1 Fanta mas.
```

–5–

They called tuna '*atun*' in Mexico because *tuna* was already reserved for the prickly pear (*Opuntia ficus-indica*). Italians called this same red cactus fruit '*fico d'India*', or 'Indian fig'. These pieces of information Jack handwrote in a pocket-sized notebook w/ a map of Rome on it. Jack wrote notes to himself as he walked along the Tiber, where there was less chance of being hit by *motorini* or *macchine*.

'Dear future self,'[6] he wrote.

If you rearrange the letters in LETTERA you can make EEL TART.

Jack then hopped a boat that went across an aqueduct bridge over the Avon + somehow ended up on the log ride at Knott's Berry Farm, circa 1973.

If we $= \Sigma$ Aui (where *Au* = authors, not gold), $\forall$ i from 1 to ∞, should a static endgame of genes be held responsible for the evolution that led to their accumulation?

'Me. We!' = shortest poem ever uttered (in 1975, when, off the cuff, a student at a Harvard lecture prompted Muhammad Ali (born Cassius Clay) for a poem). For all i = Ali.

[5] Jean Cocteau, *Beauty and the Beast: Diary of a Film* (trans. by George Amberg), New York: Dover Publications, 1972, p. 125.
[6] This font was created by digitizing the author's handwriting.

—6—

David Markson begins *Wittgenstein's Mistress* (1988) by writing, 'In the beginning, sometimes I left messages in the streets'.[7]

> JACK (V.O.)
> Fanta originated in 1940 in Germany as a Coca-Cola alternative due to the Nazi trade embargo, which affected the availability of ingredients. The modern-day formulation was 1st produced in Naples in 1955 using locally sourced oranges.

Or did Ali mean, 'Me? *Oui!*'? Or 'Me, *Wheee!*'?

In *Hopscotch* (Spanish: *Rayuela*, 1963), Julio Cortázar wrote:

> In those days it had been as if what he was writing were already laid out in front of him, writing was running a Lettera 22 over words invisible but present, like the diamond in the groove of the record.[8]

—7—

Also near the beginning of *Wittgenstein's Mistress*, the nameless (at this point) narrator dumps a VW bus full of tennis balls down the Spanish Steps in Rome.

In his 1967 essay, 'Cybernetics and Ghosts' (Italian: '*Cibernética e fantasmi*') Italo Calvino augurs the death of the author:

> What will vanish is the figure of the author, that personage to whom we persist in attributing functions that do not belong to him, the author as an exhibitor of his own soul in the permanent Exhibition of Souls, … [9]

In Joy Division's 1980 song 'Atrocity Exhibition' (named after the 1970 book by J.G. Ballard), Ian Curtis sings, 'this is the way, step inside', 16 times. Curtis died by suicide in 1980.

---

[7] David Markson, *Wittgenstein's Mistress*, Illinois: Dalkey Archive, 1990, p. 7.
[8] Julio Cortázar, *Hopscotch* (trans. Gregory Rabassa), London: Harvill, 1998, p. 430.
[9] Italo Calvino, *The Literature Machine* (trans. Patrick Creagh), London: Vintage, 1997, p. 16.

—8—

JACK (V.O.)
i used this notebook w/ Tiber Island on it for the most part to keep track of housekeeping details (literally). For example, the ghost of Beatrice Cenci lived w/ us in this attic w/ a view of the Macchina da scrivere. Cenci was beheaded in 1599 for murdering her father, who reportedly abused + raped her + other members of her family. A painting of Cenci appears repeatedly in the film Mulholland Drive + is prominently positioned between RITA (Laura Harring) + DIANE (Naomi Watts) at the 49-minute mark:

LAURA HARRING
OK, but just to see.

NAOMI WATTS
Just to see if there was an accident.

—9—

The Italian designer Bruno Munari intentionally introduced typos + mistakes in his commissioned advertisements because he believed eyes tended to gravitate towards them, compelled to correct them. As a non-commercial artist, he made a series of 'useless machines', objects which radicalized the understanding of technology + its function in the modern age.

Author's mom's ancestors were 49ers, migrating to California in search of gold. Did Au (atomic #79) want to be discovered? To be transformed from amorphous ore into valued rings + circuits that defied entropy?

—10—

If Jack tried to write 'All work and no play make Jack a dull boy' on my Lettera 22, it would come out:

```
All   or   and no pla   ma e   ac   a dull bo
```

These letters can be rearranged to write:

```
A bacon parallel, dual moon lad
```

The sequel to the Lettera 22, the Olivetti Lettera 32, was used by Francis Ford Coppola to co-write the screenplay for *The Godfather* (1972).

–11–

This 'Lettera 22' = series of love letters composed of 26 letters (+ punctuation + #s), taking 8 bits (= 1 byte) to code each letter. Character count thus far = 12,311 = 12.3 kilobytes.

–12–

Bonham Carter has 1 degree of separation w/ Bacon (they appeared together in *Novocaine* (2001)). Laura Dern also played a character in this movie, thus giving David Lynch a 'Bacon #' of 2.

i = 1 (of 8,036,077,661 + counting).

ANONYMOUS (V.O.)
i am but 1 of 8 billion who think my words are consequential enough to put in writing... but are the words themselves (unstrung together) more important than what we write about? Marshall McLuhan said something to this effect, in so many words.

'Monkey Writes' = anagram for 'New York Times'.

–13–

If you gave monkeys typewriters, how many would it take to type this?

TRACKING SHOT follows ANONYMOUS walking towards THE coliseum. Cheers echo from the ancient ruins, not of tourists but of Gladiator (2000) fans. ANON descends into the COLOSSEO metro station, running towards a sign for the CENTRAL LINE TO KIGOMA + jumping onto the moving train just as it is leaving. At 1st they are below ground, then the train emerges into the light, the same light that inspired Joseph Conrad to write 'no joy in the brilliance of sunshine.'

Anon hangs his head out the window + 3 different kids over the span of 3 minutes yell 'Chuck Norris!' when he passes, apparently the only other *mzungu* they'd seen, likely in *The Way of the Dragon* (1972), the film featuring the famous final showdown between Norris + Bruce Lee in the Colosseum.

—14—

The train lets Chuck off in Kigoma + when he tries to take a photo of the station to blog about it,[10] a cop says it is not allowed. He read in a travel book that Kigoma is where Stanley famously said, 'Livingstone, I presume.'

CUT TO: STANLEY (Spencer Tracy) squinting at a menu.

    WAITER (Sidney Poitier)
Any food allergies we should be aware of?

    STANLEY
Depends, where did you source the clams from?

    WAITER
[points to lake]
Right here, from Lake Tanganyika.

    STANLEY
In that case, i'll get the spaghetti vongole.

Both Tracy + Poitier have Bacon #s of 2.

Post-2020, 'social distance' conjures 6 feet, not degrees of separation.

---

[10] https://5cense.com/EA/Tanz_cent.htm.

—15—

While iii waitted for my congolese, iipulled out myMacBook. Not that i had annything in particular towrite about, but ii felt self-conscious sitttinngtthere alone. iiii typed '1 Fantamas' on my Buttterfly keyboard, which was too quiet formy ttastes + kept sttickiinng on certain lettters + the spacebar diidn'twork ½ thettime sothe wordsrantogether. Nevertheless, tthiis MacBook + IlnDesign software wantme tokeep tttyping b/c ittjustiiifies their creation + continued proliiiiiiferattiion, though i suspectthis Buttterfly keyboard will 1 daybe rendered obsolette.

Thiskeyboard wants me ttocontinue wriiting thestory aboutt goiiingto the Fanta storewhen ii was 11, but iacciidenttally typed 'mas Fanta' intothe searchwindow + wasnow presentted w/ opttiions to BUY Fanta. Most siites displayed the uglynew plastiicbotttles, but idid see an optionto buy the Mexiican glass-botttled type w/ribbed ridgesthat helpedto grip, the kind ii rememberedas akid.

—16—

[Edited after the fact] Reading the fine print on 1 site, it appears the original formulation used only ingredients available in Germany at the time, including beets, whey + apple pomace—the 'leftovers of leftovers'. During WWII, Fanta was not necessarily consumed as a beverage but was used in cooking to add sweetness + flavor to soups + stews, as sugar was rationed.

—17—

CUT TO: JAMES JOYCE (Rupert Friend), emerging from the COLOSSEO station onto a street lined w/ women sitting at tables w/ typewriters.

JOYCE
Vorrei scrivere 1 lettera a mio fratello, puoi scriverlo in inglese?

TYPIST (Sophia Loren)
Yessir, yessir, 30 lira per word.

JOYCE
[counting words as he says them]
Dear Stanislaus,
[motions typist to do carriage return]
Rome reminds me of a man who lives by exhibiting to travellers his grandmother's corpse.

JOYCE counts out 500 lira + hands it to the typist in exchange for the letter.

–18–

Cormac McCarthy used a Lettera 32 to write nearly all of his fiction, screenplays + correspondence, totalling (by his estimate) more than 5,000,000 words. The Lettera 32 that he purchased in 1963 was auctioned in 2009 to an unidentified collector for $254,500. McCarthy then paid $11 for a replacement typewriter of the same model, but in newer condition.

–19–

It's hard to account for how many words i've written on my Lettera 22—most of what i've typed is to make concrete poetry.

Full disclaimer: This or should be filed under fiction since i never o ned a Lettera 22. Ho ever, a Remington / an Italian e board did o n me for a spell. The machine in the aforementioned photo (in the shado of Mussolini's T pe riter) is in fact this t pe riter. The font in this paragraph as created b digitizing the output of said Remington. I named it Romington, a nod to Remus + Romulus, the auguring t in brothers ho ere born on Tiber Island. Under the guise of Rem+Rom, i used this font to rite parts of *A Raft Manifest* (ISBN: 978-1-940853-09-3).

–20–

The author of this text was born 11/22/66. Mark Ruffalo was born on 11/22/67. Scarlett Johansson was born on 11/22/84 . Both Ruffalo + Johansson have a Bacon # of 1 (+ have appeared together in films, does that make their Bacon # 0?).

Mariel Hemingway was born 11/22/61 + Terry Gilliam was born on 11/22/40: both have Bacon #s of 2. 'A haywire lemming' is an anagram for Mariel Hemingway.

JFK was shot on 11/22/63.

–21–

My 1st 2 cars were made in the year i was born, a '66 Ford Mustang + a '66 VW Bug. i bought the Bug for $50 + sold it a few years later for $50. It may have had a bumper sticker that read: 'My karma ran over my dogma'.

I don't remember what i paid for the Italian Remington that i bought at the Porta Portese flea market in Rome, but i recently sold it for $75 on Craigslist.

–22–

A: «Me Ali, you Emmi» grunted Ali (El Hedi ben Salem), in effect, in the R.W. Fassbinder film *Ali: Fear Eats the Soul* (1974). «Which Fassbinder film is it?» asks Laurie Anderson in her concert film, *Home of the Brave* (1986). «The 1-armed man comes into a flower shop + says, 'What flower expresses days go by?'»

B: Books are standalone technology that require nothing else to read them. Ditto typewriters, swapping read for write (+ adding paper + fresh ribbons).

C: They drive us, not vice versa.

D: W.E.B. Du Bois coined the term «double consciousness» to describe the sense of always looking at 1-self through the eyes of others, in addition to just being 1's self.

E: In *The Trouble With Being Born* (1973), E.M. Cioran wrote: «It is not worth the bother of killing yourself, since you always kill yourself too late.»

F: Even the broken Fanta bottles we recycled. We'd break them into shards + cement them to the tops of walls, poor man's barbed wire. The bottlecaps we used to nail down tarpaper in our chicken coop.

G: «Glib jocks quiz nymph to vex dwarf» = 28-letter pangram using all letters of the English alphabet.

H: 1 can't quote from *A Humument* (1970) without quoting from the remaindered Victorian novel Tom Phillips «treated» to make it.

i: $\forall$ = «for all» in mathematical terms, why author's name = $\forall$ i, an accumulation of all i've read before.

L: If you rearrange the letters in «LETTERS» you can spell «SETTLER» or «LET REST». If a proofreader wants to indicate that a previous edit should be ignored they write «STET», which in Latin means «let it stand».

M: Marshall McLuhan is credited w/ saying «we shape our tools and thereafter they shape us» in the '60s, but in 1943 Winston Churchill said «we shape our buildings; thereafter they shape us.»

N: Word count thus far = 3,489, but does this count #s + standalone letters? + footnotes? Character count = 19,920 (= 20 kb in source code), counting spaces.

O: In 1959, the Lettera 22 was picked as best product design of the century by the IIT (Illinois Institute of Technology).

P: *Fantasma* = phantom in both Italian + Spanish.

Q: « »

R: Even further back, in 1854, Thoreau Wrote: «We do not ride the railroad; it rides upon us.»

S: Both Spanish + English pluralize by adding s.

T: Thoreau also said «men have become the tools of their tools.»

U: Umberto Eco penned the Italian (no J, K, W, X or Y) pangram: «Berlusconi? Quiz, tv, paghe da fame.»

V: *De burro* or *de vaca*?

W: «Double-U» looks like «double-V» (VV) + ME flipped upside-doWn = WE. *Ouui!*

Z:

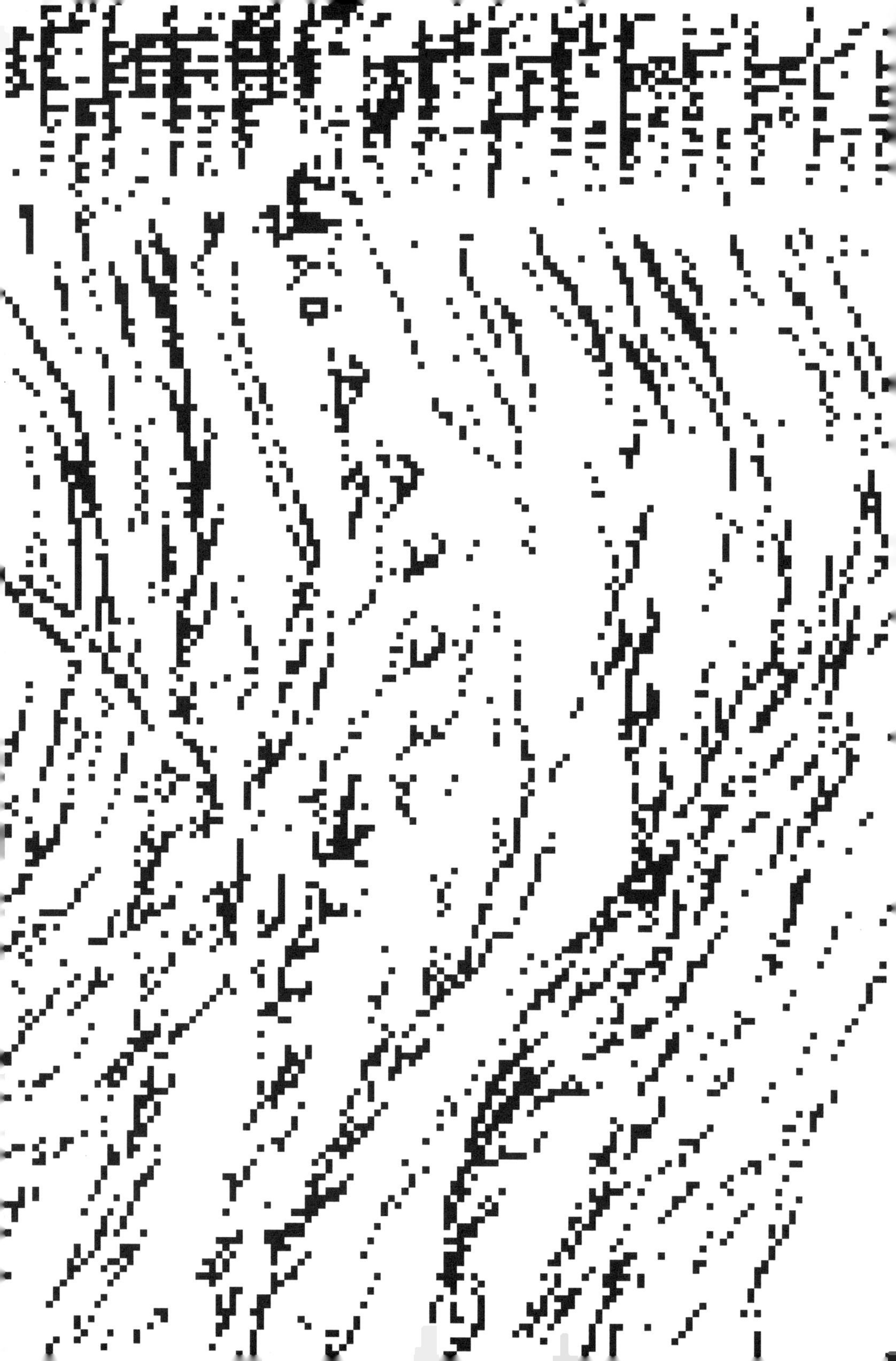

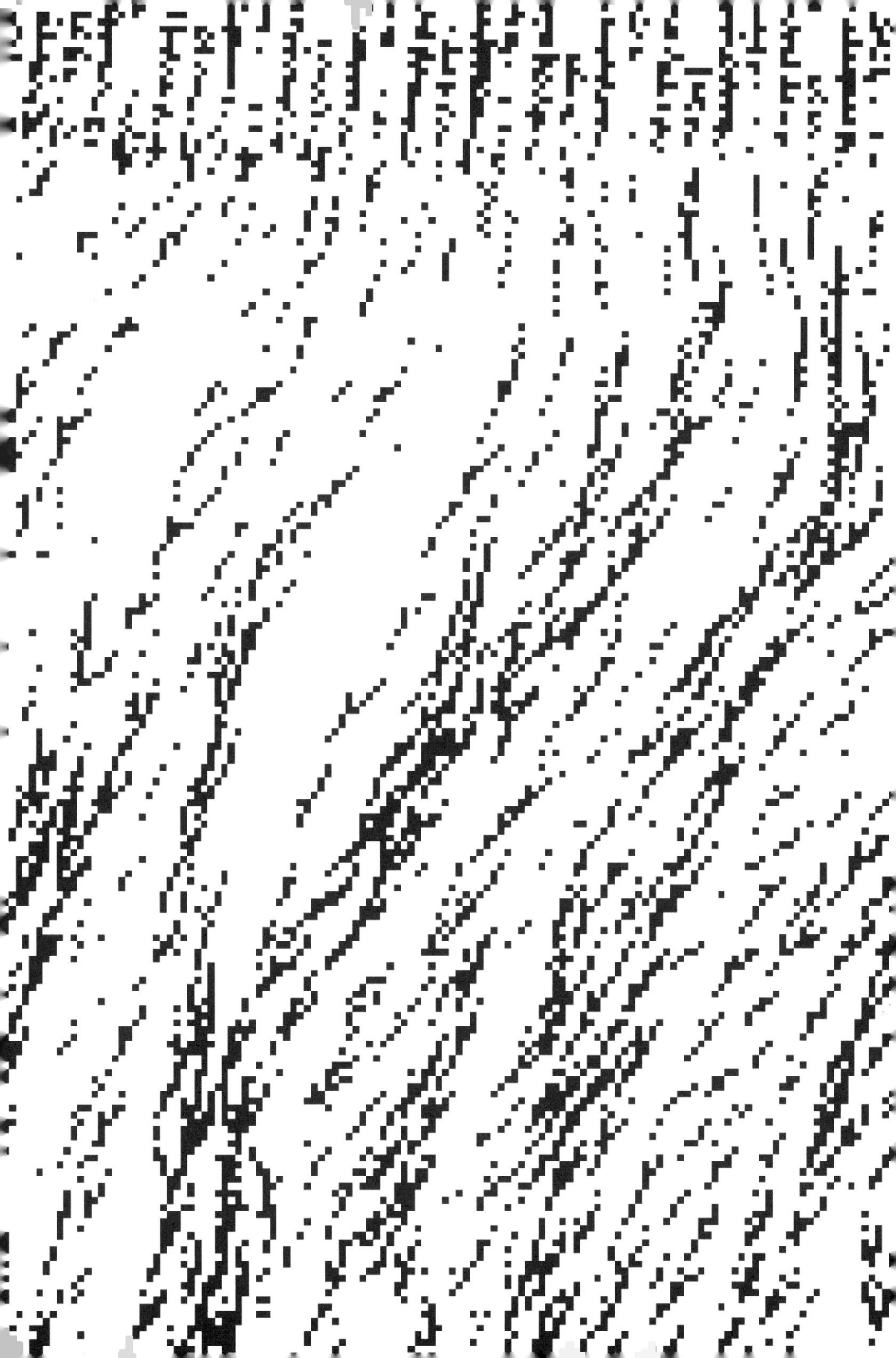

TOUCH
JAG
LISA HSI

N AND
AR

O CHEN

Toucan and Jaguar

Lisa Hsiao Chen

I met him at a party. This was years ago. I can't remember how many exactly. I'm not good with time.

The party had a name. Forgive it: If on a Winter's Night a Party. *Please come in costumes inspired by the writings of Italo Calvino.*

I lived, back then, in a small midwestern town, the farthest I'd ever been from an ocean. The local college had invited me to be a fellow. I loved being a fellow. Highly recommend. First, you demonstrate your talents. Then, you're gone before your shine starts to dim.

I also loved, still love, theme parties. Some people are repelled by them. They resent being poked at with a stick to have fun.

Why can't I have a drink and a cigarette and just talk to people in peace, they say.

For me, the people who grumble the loudest about theme parties are the least likely to feel truly free in their skins.

Freedom without obligation is a particular kind of American loneliness, the kind that fools you into thinking you're happy.

I spent hours fabricating a toucan headdress from colored paper. I arrived alone.

I knew the husband of the couple who hosted the party. That night, he was incarnated as Kubla Khan. I recall his armor: a stainless-steel steamer basket flattened against his chest.

His wife, a tiny woman with watery blue eyes, was – of course – Marco Polo. French, she kissed me on both cheeks. A red beret sloped from her head like a vintage rubber hot-water bottle.

At some point in the evening, I found myself in the kitchen, wedged in the narrow space between the sink and the stove. The party had reached its peak. A few glasses had been broken; people shouted to hear one another above the swell of music and laughter.

I stood triangulated between Mr Palomar in a shabby overcoat, his neck draped with a wreath of oyster mushrooms, and a woman who, despite the February chill, was wearing a bikini top and flowing skirt. She was the mortified Signora Isotta Barbarino from 'The Adventure of a Bather', unwilling to come ashore because she'd lost the bottom half of her bathing suit in the ocean.

A man in cat ears approached and tried to maneuver around us. He'd spilled something, he apologized, and needed the sink. Mr Palomar, irked by the interruption, stopped cold in the middle of his point about Kurosawa's use of chiaroscuro.

The signora took the opportunity to adjust her outfit. She was in extraordinary physical shape – achieved, I surmised, through a punishing regimen of daily fitness. She possessed none of the fictional signora's timorous, sweet plumpness, or her fretfulness over the betrayal of her body.

It was in these short minutes of shifting choreography that my jaguar and I, two strangers, recognized each other. Even though his shirt was technically leopard print, I knew instantly he was the jaguar to my toucan.

We'd each drawn our inspiration from a Calvino lecture in which a toucan and a jaguar appear as bit players, plopped onto the stage of narrative, eternally on the verge of being recombined and coded into language.

My jaguar was not good-looking. His mouth was wide and rubbery and set too close to his nose, which made his face seem crumpled, like someone missing a lot of teeth. Yet in his eyes I thought I glimpsed something both tender and rough and ultimately dismantling. There lay the darkness of his beauty: in his eyes and in how he moved.

I observed him arrange and rearrange himself. He crossed his legs at his ankles. He ballasted himself, placing his paws on the lip of the sink behind him. He shook the hair from his eyes.

I know this sounds like nothing.

It's possible my intense watchfulness couldn't, at that moment, be separated from the exquisite agony of sensing that once this interval of oblivious chatter between Palomar and Isotta had run its course, we would, at last, have an opening to begin our pas de deux.

Kurosawa was a maniac, the signora was saying. He had his crew spend hours spraying acres of grass with gold paint, just to get the glint right for a nighttime scene. And then he left it all on the cutting room floor!

Mr Palomar chuckled. Whatever it takes, he said, fingering his mushrooms. I mean, he's a true auteur, after all. Whatever it takes.

❦

After the term of my fellowship ended, I stayed in the little town for my jaguar. I continued my research into psycholinguistics and feral children.

My jaguar worked several jobs. One of them involved teaching puppet-making classes to senior citizens in nursing homes. He had some background in theater, but his further attempts to interest the seniors in staging puppet plays were not successful.

The senior citizens did not stick with their scripts. They preferred to improvise.

Through their puppets, the senior citizens revealed their woes. In wee voices or gruff voices, the puppets described their unhappiness with their surroundings, or how they sometimes felt sodden or confused.

The seniors listened to their own puppets with kind forbearance. There, there, they said. Hush now, they said.

These puppet shows, I remember telling my jaguar, reminded me of little girls when they play mommy with their dolls. A strangely sinister quality would, on occasion, creep into their solemn mimicry.

I didn't grow up with old people. I grew up in a community of refugees where hardly anyone was older than fifty. I didn't know how to be around them. Old people to me were white and sometimes casually racist, even if they meant no harm. Mostly, it seemed, they wanted me to know, over and over, how lucky I was.

My jaguar said, Oh don't be so hard on people, Fruit Loops.

He said he liked working with senior citizens. When people get very old, they shed their cunning and their social graces and become more who they actually are and perhaps have always been.

But why is that good? I asked. I didn't say: Shame and cunning have made me who I am.

The puppetry program had barely any budget for materials. The puppets were often little more than colorful socks with glued-on eyes. My jaguar, too, was broke. Worse, he seemed not to mind and to even consider his penury an ethical lifestyle!

As a child, I was once given a puppet turtle from a family friend. I was not unused to playing by myself. But with my hand snaked into the puppet's satin interior, I found my imagination deflated and my solitude magnified. Soon after, I had occasion to regift the puppet for a classmate's birthday, which pleased my parents because it meant they didn't have to spend any money. Privately, I told myself I was giving the turtle another chance at life.

Even when in the company of others, the jaguar is a solitary creature. The toucan is social.

The whole time my jaguar and I were together, I admit, I hoped to lure him out of his little town. But it became clear he could not truly exist outside the only habitat he'd ever known.

The town assured him of who he was in the world. His family had been there for generations, passing on their cars, addictions and shrinking plots of land. In this manner the pattern on the coat of the jaguar evolved to mirror the dapple of sunlight through the overstory.

My mother was happy for me. She enjoyed hearing about my life of nothingness. Her own life had proven to her that, more important than happiness, was safety.

My father made a hobby of researching houses for sale in the town where the jaguar and I lived. He liked to click through all the rooms online and shake his head at the marble kitchens.

So cold! Like a place where food goes to die, he said.

I didn't know where my home was anymore, but for sure it wasn't this little town.

Lisa Hsiao Chen

I found myself jotting in my notebook: *Would we still be together had we not met as Toucan and Jaguar, the sprocket and chain of fables and myths?*

And: *Our lives here in this little town – is this the best we can do? Wrong to blame the little town, not its fault?*

My jaguar moved very softly through the forest. So quiet you sometimes forgot he was there. We lasted a little more than a year.

I'm telling you all this now because I returned to the little town recently to give a short talk. Two decades had passed since that party. Hardly anyone I knew still lived there.

Kubla Khan, I'd heard through the grapevine, died of bone cancer some years ago; Marco Polo had dissolved into weepy alcoholism and moved out west to dry out.

After my talk I retreated to my hotel room, worn out by my public persona. I'd booked an early flight the next morning. I kicked off my shoes and lay in bed.

Whenever I travel, it's my habit to pick up the local paper. It's a way of slipping into the timestream of a place, like tuning into a talk-radio station on a road trip and listening until it eventually crackles out of range, leaving you with the floating sensation of having crossed minor galaxies.

I scanned the usual stories about teenage car crashes and controversial planning commission votes.

It was in the community calendar that I found, below an item about a fundraiser for an animal shelter, a notice for something called Death Cafe.

The bimonthly meeting was scheduled for later that very night. My jaguar's name was listed as the facilitator.

I was the last to arrive at the basement of a church on the edge of town where the Death Cafe was meeting. A boxed coffee dispenser and Chessmen butter cookies had been set out on a folding table. A heating unit – ancient, insufficient – roared.

Six people sat together in a circle. Among them was my jaguar. His eyes grew wide when he saw me. Like me, he had thickened around the waist, and elsewhere, lost the careless luster of youth. Still, he held himself with the aristocratic languor of an apex predator. His dark eyes glittered.

As I slipped into an empty chair, my jaguar continued with his introductory remarks.

Death Cafe was founded more than a decade ago by an Englishman.

Death Cafe is not a grief support group. There are other places to go for that. It's a space to have open, informal conversations about death.

There are no experts here, my jaguar said. Death belongs to everybody. We're here because we have one thing in common: we're all going to die.

My jaguar asked the group if there was anything on their mind they wanted to share.

No one spoke.

Okay then, my jaguar said, leaning forward in his chair. What about something that's been in the news lately? Is anyone following the assisted suicide debate in Massachusetts?

A man who had been sitting with his arms crossed and resting above his belly coughed and raised his hand in the manner of a seasoned bidder at an estate auction.

Speaking of the euthanization of the self, the man said. Who here is familiar with the Sarco pod?

A few of us shook our heads.

It's new, a real breakthrough, the man said. Dutch or Swiss, I think. Basically, you climb into this thing that looks like a spaceship. Then you push a button that releases nitrogen gas. And boom, it's over in less than ten minutes.

The wild-eyed woman next to me lifted her chin, regal. I'd do that in an instant. I mean, if it came to that. She stared at the group. Why should we punish ourselves and others with our pain?

But, but... what if you change your mind? This, from a woman swaddled in a wool scarf and what looked like a pussyhat.

The conversation turned to issues of legality and the ethics of monetization and access. My jaguar, who seemed to be up on the latest Sarco news, said the pod wasn't designed to be sold. The idea was to make a blueprint freely available so anyone could make a capsule of their own with a 3D printer.

Lisa Hsiao Chen

It's a time *release* capsule, Pussyhat tittered, then looked down remorsefully at her feet.

The talk shifted to the future of Sarcos for pets. I listened, not without interest. Every time my gaze became momentarily entangled with my jaguar's, I felt my cheeks flush before one of us looked away.

I had come for a reason.

I suppose I wanted to see what would happen next in the story of my jaguar and me, if I had to put it into words.

My mind drifted to our first meeting, cramped between the kitchen sink and the stove, that quiet snow tunnel we'd dug within the din of the party so we could reach each other, how we had waited for our time to begin.

There seemed to be no such snow tunnel in that church basement that night. There was nothing but open tundra and unspeakable, dark shapes I couldn't identify.

I knew then that I had to make my exit before the bathroom break. I had to leave here before then, so as not to be trapped in conversation. I allowed another 35 minutes to pass before I rose from my seat. I feinted demurely in the direction of the toilets, and fled the building.

꜃

That night in bed, I lay very stiff and pretended I was in a Sarco pod. I had no interest in dying. But I was curious to know what it would feel like to have command over the last hour before my future's eclipse.

I imagined a send-off where my pod would be ejected into the open ocean. In the manner of a whale fall, my pod and my carcass would biodegrade into a food buffet for legions of deep-sea creatures.

Adrift in the balm of my imaginary death chamber, it came to me, this thought: It was not within my power to foreclose on the story of Toucan and Jaguar. So long as my jaguar and I lived and breathed the page would turn, the film would keep rolling, the curtain would not fall. So long as I continued to preen and my jaguar to scratch himself, so long as I yawned and daydreamed and he cried out in his sleep or lifted an ass cheek to release a fart, so long as we existed in time and were capable of leaving fresh marks on it, our story would not end on this winter's night, not in a church basement with a group of strangers over sour cups of coffee, not tomorrow either, or the week after that; it would keep seeping through door cracks and scraping against the windowpane, the story of Toucan and

Jaguar; it would pool from the ceiling, buckle the concrete; it would scorch the forest in furious pursuit of our fates, until there remained just one of us, the one alone with a puppet, the puppet of the one who is gone.

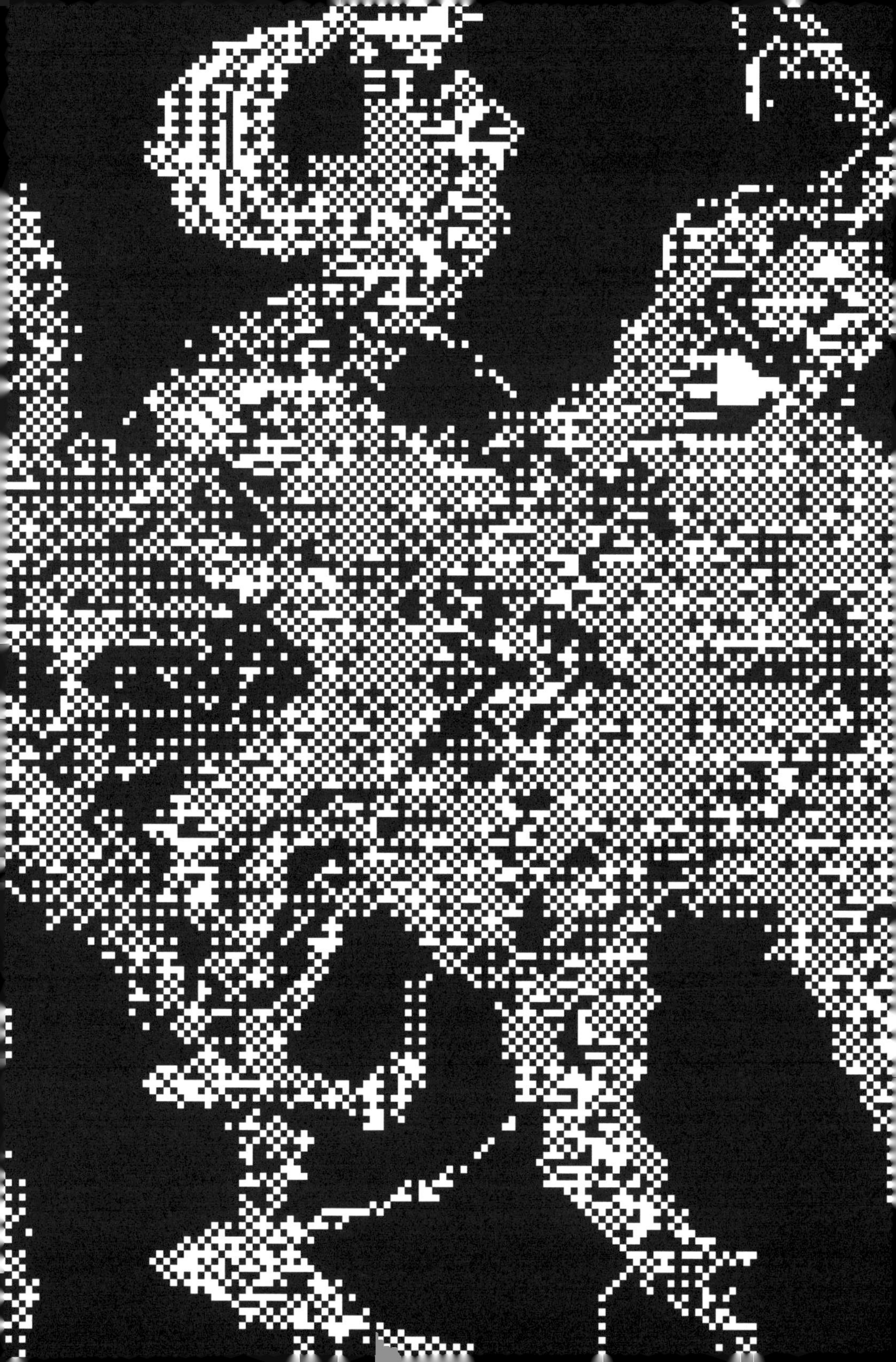

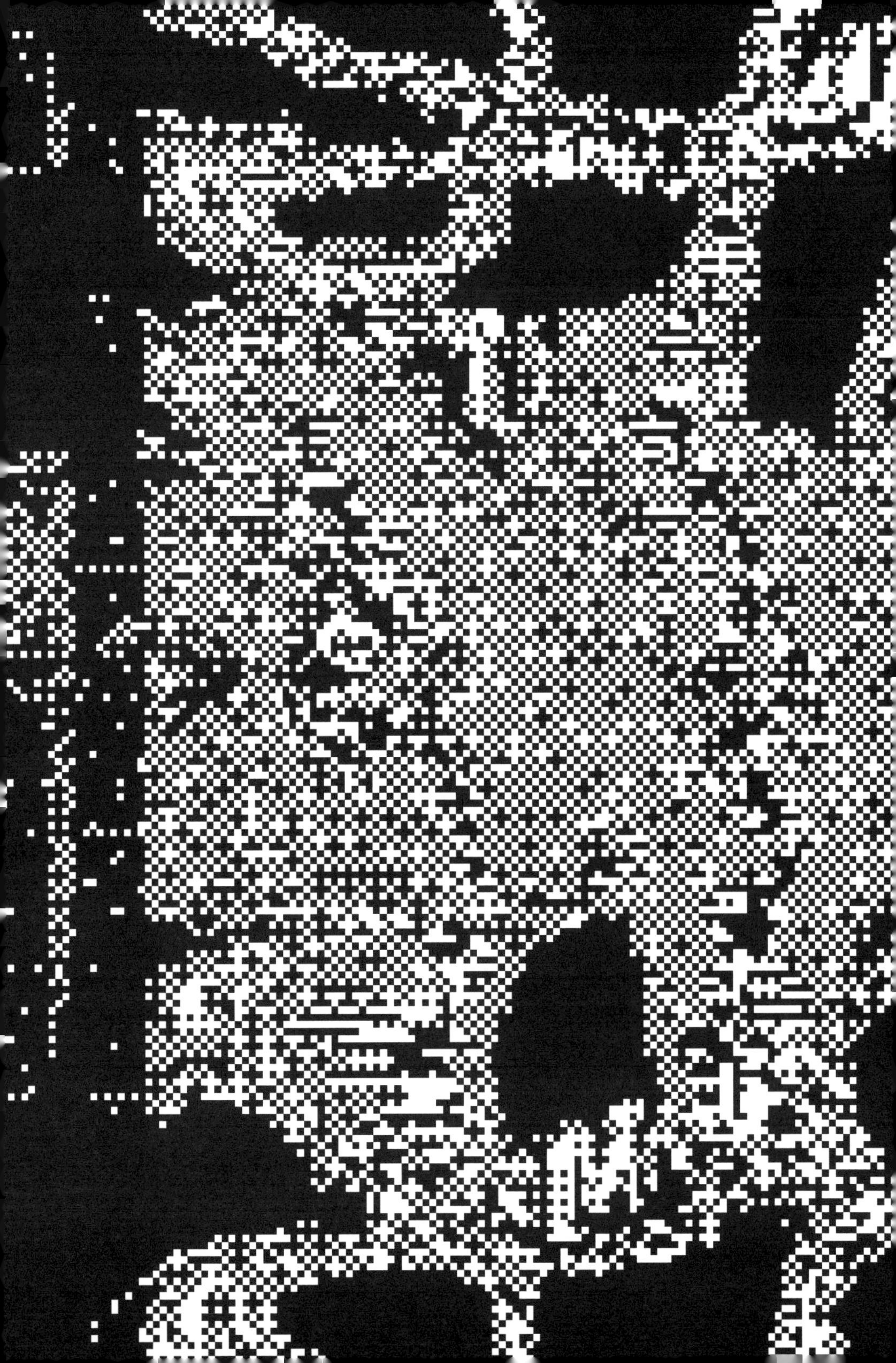

THE GH
THE AI
GEOI
MORI

OST OF
RICOT
FREY
ISON

The Ghost of the Apricot

Geoffrey Morrison

My brother is piping up on the ridge. There is sun on the ridge and so I can hardly see him. There is wind on the ridge and so I can hardly hear him. There is sun on the grass and on the coats of the sheep and in the stream that runs down from the ridge and far out into the green and golden distance until it disappears somewhere in the woods. Naturally, there is also sun in the sky, but because of the wind there are few clouds, and they are thin clouds, like white wool carded almost to nothing. Or so I assume. The carding of wool is not exactly my business. It is not exactly my brother's business, either. In two or three weeks we will bring these sheep into the village to be shorn. Someone — not us — will card the wool, and spin it, and dye it, and knit it, and tailor it, and wear it. In the meantime we will have collected our wages from the man who pays us and brought the sheep back out to the grass and the stream and the ridge to watch the wool grow until it is time to do it all over again.

The ones who card and spin are women. I am a woman but I do not card and spin. I herd. This is how it is and how I like it. My brother doesn't mind it, either. Most of the time, we get along fine. When we don't get along fine, he says, 'May God shit on you, won't you go off and get married again already?' Perhaps I will go off and get married again, but if I do I will be sure to marry a shepherd. Last time I did not, and that was my mistake. One of my mistakes. So until I find an acceptable shepherd to go off with, I live with my brother and watch the wool grow with him.

My brother's melody is wild and sad. Wild, but skilled — a wildness only ever reached by the truly skilled. Or the truly sad. It sounds like a wind that has raced to the ends of the earth and back, and seen everything there is to see, and known everything there is to know, and still it shrieks in a defeated rage at all it does not have and cannot be. It is all the sadder because this poor shrieking melody-wind is small and hard to hear in the real wind that huffs away quite happily without noticing my brother. When my brother plays such a melody, there is a good chance we are about to enter a period of not getting along.

'Brother,' I think, 'give your lips a break. You will need them in good shape for when that pious nun comes up here again.' But for all I know he plays this whirling lament because she will not come up here anymore. I've told them both a hundred times that they are dicing with the devil, and maybe they've finally had the sense to see it. But if they have finally had the sense to see it then he surely resents me now for being right, and unless I do something to calm him we will certainly enter a period of not getting along.

I climb the ridge and go into the cottage to collect my bow and strings. I see the embers in the hearth, the rough wooden table, and the heavy purple curtain that divides my sleeping area from my brother's. We keep the cottage clean, but we can never truly banish the odour of smoky stones. My instrument is close to my bed. I keep it wrapped in a sheepskin of its own, as if it were a baby sleeping next to me. It is about the size of a baby. It is the shape of a pear. A pear is a baby of the pear tree, and it brings me a strange happiness to know that my instrument was made from pear wood. Not all of them are.

Of course, it was not always my instrument. It was my husband's. This instrument is the only thing he gave me which I was glad to receive, not least because when he gave it to me he was dead. My instrument is pear wood and my brother's flute is apricot wood, so that when we play together it is as the child of the pear and the child of the apricot. Or the ghost of the pear. The ghost of the apricot. Sometimes I forget that the trees from which our instruments were made are also dead.

I sweep my bow across the strings as once the breeze swept the branches, and my notes rise into the air as once the pears fell to the earth. The pears would be eaten or would grow into new trees or would rot. My notes are heard or not heard. If they are not heard, do they rot? Where is the rain to wash away a rotten note? Time, I suppose, is the answer. The rain of time. I stare at the stones that have sheltered us so many seasons. I am beginning to frighten myself.

Back outside, my brother is still battling the wind with his whirling melody. The lungs on that man. Without saying anything, I turn over the bucket I use on such occasions, sit down next to him, and stand my instrument at my knee. He is in his own world, and so my first task will be to join him there.

I close my eyes and listen carefully. The ghost of the apricot tries to be the wind, but today the wind is the wind, and there is his problem. One of his problems. I think of the smoke-scented stones. I think of the hearth I have left quietly glowing since this morning, ready to be stoked back into fire when I cook for us tonight. I think of the thin grey ribbon of smoke that leaves our chimney from such embers, as if God himself were playing with a little piece of wool no one wanted anymore, stretching it up into the sky as far as it could go. If the ghost of the apricot tries to be the wind, the ghost of the pear will be smoke.

And what does smoke do in the wind? It winds. It bends. It trails. And so I do it, rising rough and sinuous into an air that blasts me hither and yon. I know I am playing well. Lord knows what my brother knows. The more I join him, the more his playing seems confused, distracted. This is not what I had hoped for. I see I must sing him a story — something already known and something not yet known. I will know it in the singing. This is always how it is.

There will be death in this story. That much I know. Up on the ridge, in the loneliness of storms, the tales of death are our sole consolation. I know it and my brother knows it. We hardly know why. But I like this thought and so I make it the first lines of my song:

> Up on the ridge
> In the loneliness of storms
> The tales of death
> Are our sole consolation

I need more now. I have sparked the fire and now it needs air. Air may seem meaningless, nothingness, but it gets us going and gives me time to think up what's next. I see no reason to stray from the formula that has served me so well before:

> Ancestors in graves
> Ancestors in unmarked places
> In the depths of the woods
> At the bottom of the sea
> Arise and say again what you have seen
>
> Say so we may know
> How you have lived
> Say so we may know
> How to die

I am disciplining the wind. His playing has become steadier, though for the moment also less inspired. Good enough.

    I know as I call out to the dead for advice that I must not sing a tale of a shepherd. We are shepherds, and so we know what it is like. Songs of shepherds are for people in towns. What's more, I will make things worse if I sing a tale that reminds my brother too directly of his woes. I have heard from travelling people a beautiful song of a shepherd whose heart is torn out and eaten by three women. It is not a song about women's evil. It is a song about women's power. The song has the magic of the moon, and when I think it to myself I am reminded what it is to be alive. But if I sing this now, and the shepherd for whom I sing is grieving the condition of his heart in the teeth of a nun who will no longer come here, then we may permanently enter a period of not getting along. It is too great a risk. I must catch the magic of the moon in the song of the eaten heart and let it fill a song on a different theme. I must pour an old, fine wine into new skins.

> Snow on the mountains

I sing,

> But spring in the valleys
> And spring in the heart
> Of the bandit king

> On rides a man
> Who is happy and heedless
> Landless and nameless
> And free

There are many old formulas. Formulas about snow, about mountains, about valleys, about bandit kings. Sly bandit kings, leering, gallant, cowardly, generous, wretched. Bandit kings on horses, on donkeys, in ox-carts, on rafts going down the river. I have heard them from old singers and made them my own. And so, rising on the smoke of my notes like scraps of paper, come formulas and elements, incidents and types, known from before but combined in new ways not yet known.

And so I sing of a free bandit king riding a wild red roan in springtime: a king, in fact, of nothing — his men have departed from him, his women also, and yet he glories in sunlight and clear mountain water and cares not that no one now follows him. The bandit king guards his saddlebag jealously. There may be something inside that is the key to his happiness even now, alone in the high green valleys. There may be something inside that is key to his aloneness, so that he is happy in spite of what he carries, not because of it. Or there may be something inside that is simply a key, a key to somewhere else no better or worse than before, only different. I do not yet know what the bandit king has in his saddlebag. It will become what it is only when the bag opens, and it will open only when everything else I sing has made it impossible for it not to. There is a chance it won't open at all. And though at this moment I do not know the nature of this hidden thing, I must act like I do. That is the secret to a good song. Though I am making it all up as I go along, I can never let this be known. It all must seem a thousand years old and true.

So here he is, solitary brigand-boss on a horse. I said he was nameless, so for the time being let's keep him that way. Giving a name to a nameless person is an act somewhat akin to revealing the nature of a key. He sleeps under a heavy sheepskin, in woods and on ridges and in open fields. He hides with care the traces of his camps. He eats what he can catch, pick, pluck, tear out, or steal. In the meantime my brother and I have ceased to be wind and smoke. The ghost of the pear and the ghost of the apricot now inhabit the forms of living pears, living apricots. My brother's melody on the apricot wood is sweet but hard, like a pear. My embellishments on the pear wood are soft but bitter, like an apricot. Now he is me, and I am he. Contraries are good in music and good in stories and good in songs. So far, then, so good.

In a moment something needs to happen. Something contrary. But before I can sing it, my brother stops playing. He looks down the ridge in the direction of the woods that swallow up the stream. He holds up a hand and I stop, too. But the grass, the stream, and the edge of the woods are still just grass, stream, edge of woods.

'What did you see?' I ask him. I am afraid of his answer. I am afraid it will be something only he can see.

'I think…', he begins. 'No, I saw. A wolf. It had something in its mouth. Black cloth.' He says this with the same dispassion he would use to describe rain clouds creeping down to us from the mountains. But I know he is thinking of his nun. Without another word between us, we go into the cottage and put away our instruments. Though it is warm, we put on heavy leather gloves. I take a long wooden staff. My brother takes the axe we use to split firewood. We have killed wolves before with these tools. The trick is to keep it at bay with the staff, knock it back when it lunges, and deliver the killing blow with the axe before it can recover itself. It is a two-person job. Like music, I suppose. Or like love, though I was always more skilled at music. Killing a wolf is more bloody than music. Perhaps no less bloody than love.

We usually avoid the woods. All but the stupidest sheep avoid them, too. Of course, there are many songs involving incidents in dangerous woods. There are even a certain number of songs involving the mistaken belief that a beloved has died after the discovery of a veil torn by animals. The lover of the beloved is inevitably so stricken by grief that they kill themselves, only for the unharmed beloved to discover the dead lover and, of course, kill themselves. I don't like these songs very much. Bad woodcraft. Any true hunter or shepherd or swineherd or milkmaid knows that a sign is not the same as the thing itself. My brother knows too, or at least he usually does, when he is master of himself, which is not always. I watch him carefully as we step through wet deadfall. I may have to remind him of the stupid songs of the animal-torn veils to keep him from despairing too soon. Perhaps that is the real purpose of such songs — to shake someone out of a premature despair by showing them that they are being stupid. Certainly they have been around a long time, these songs, and so have stupidity and despair. One such song is so old it has lions in it. I have never seen a lion. I heard from a wise man, or at least a learned man, or at least a priest, that there used to be lions here, or near here, even for a few hundred years after the birth of Christ. I do not know if things once true hundreds of years ago may suddenly become true again. Matters of hundreds of years are for the wise, or at least the learned, or at least the priests. My matters are songs and seasons.

    We stay quiet as we step deeper into the woods. Some beasts must be made aware of your arrival and other beasts already know you are there; it is this second kind of beast one must listen for. Wolves are this second kind of beast. I do not know what kind lions are. We are so quiet I can hear individual leaves twitching on the trees. We are so quiet I can hear the snapping sound when one of these leaves loosens from its branch and falls to earth. My brother's face is serious. We take turns in the lead. We look for tracks, for shit, for blood, for fur. We see nothing. We lose sight of the stream. An hour passes this way, or what feels like an hour. It will be sunset soon, and our flock has been unguarded for too long. This was a foolhardy idea. We should go back. But just as I think this I see a thinning in the oncoming trees, a thinning and then bright rays of late afternoon light. We have reached the other side of the woods. We have never been to the other side of the woods — there was never anything for us there, never any need. I see a ridge and a grassy valley and a stream much like the one where we stay. Very much like. It may even be the same stream. I turn to say this to my brother but my brother is not there. I call for my brother. I step a few paces back into the woods and look for my brother. I say, 'May God shit on you, this is not funny!', but do not roust my brother. He is nowhere. I am not frightened yet. I know my way back, more or less. Perhaps someone lives up on this ridge just as we do on ours. Perhaps this person has seen my brother. Perhaps this person has seen the nun. Perhaps this person has seen the wolf.

    I climb the ridge. There are no sheep in this valley and I do not believe whoever lives up there is a shepherd. But I know someone must. I can see the smoke. The wind has picked up again and is beginning to tease at it, card it apart like grey wool in a sky now almost sunset. I must have misjudged the time. I do not see how I will return home before dark. Perhaps they will let me stay the night here. But as I come closer I see there is no *here* to stay the night, not really. There is no cottage. The smoke rises from a dying fire set in a small circle of stones. A campsite for a traveller, though no traveller can be seen. Next to the fire is a heavy, yellowing, weather-worn sheepskin. It smells of smoke and horse and masculine sweat. The sweat of a man long out alone on the road, a crownless king, a nameless key. Next to the sheepskin is a garment of heavy black cloth, neatly folded, of the kind a nun would wear. It is spotless, perhaps newly washed, perhaps even lately perfumed in the oils and balms of a distant and high-spired city on a sunny sea. Resting in the folds of the garment are two little piles of fruits, soft and bright and fresh off the tree. Pears and apricots. It is strange. It is not quite the season for either, or at least they are not in season on the other side of the woods. Next to the garment is an upturned wooden bucket, and on this bucket is a heavy open book. The pages turn in the wind. Matters of books are like matters of hundreds of years. I cannot read them. They are for the wise, or at least the learned, or at least the priests. My matters are songs and seasons. But the turning stops on a page with pictures, and although pictures are not among my matters they may show matters which are mine. These pictures are all in a row: a lion with gore-smeared lips mauls the veil of the beloved; the lover discovers the bloody veil and, in despair, takes up the knife; the beloved discovers the bloody body of the lover and, in a despair no less total, does the same. In this last picture, the poor lion watches from behind a rock with an expression at once contrite and curious. He did not know. He did not mean for this. He had not wanted to be author of a story that unfolds forever in the pictures on the page and the neat lines of letters beneath it that I cannot read and the familiar formulas of songs, songs whose notes rise from the ghosts of pears and the ghosts of apricots and rot in the rains of time.

    Next to the book is a saddlebag with a buckled pouch. I take off my gloves, unbuckle it, and reach in my hand. My bow hand. The blood is warm. I smell ashes of trees that are no longer trees on a wind that is still the wind.

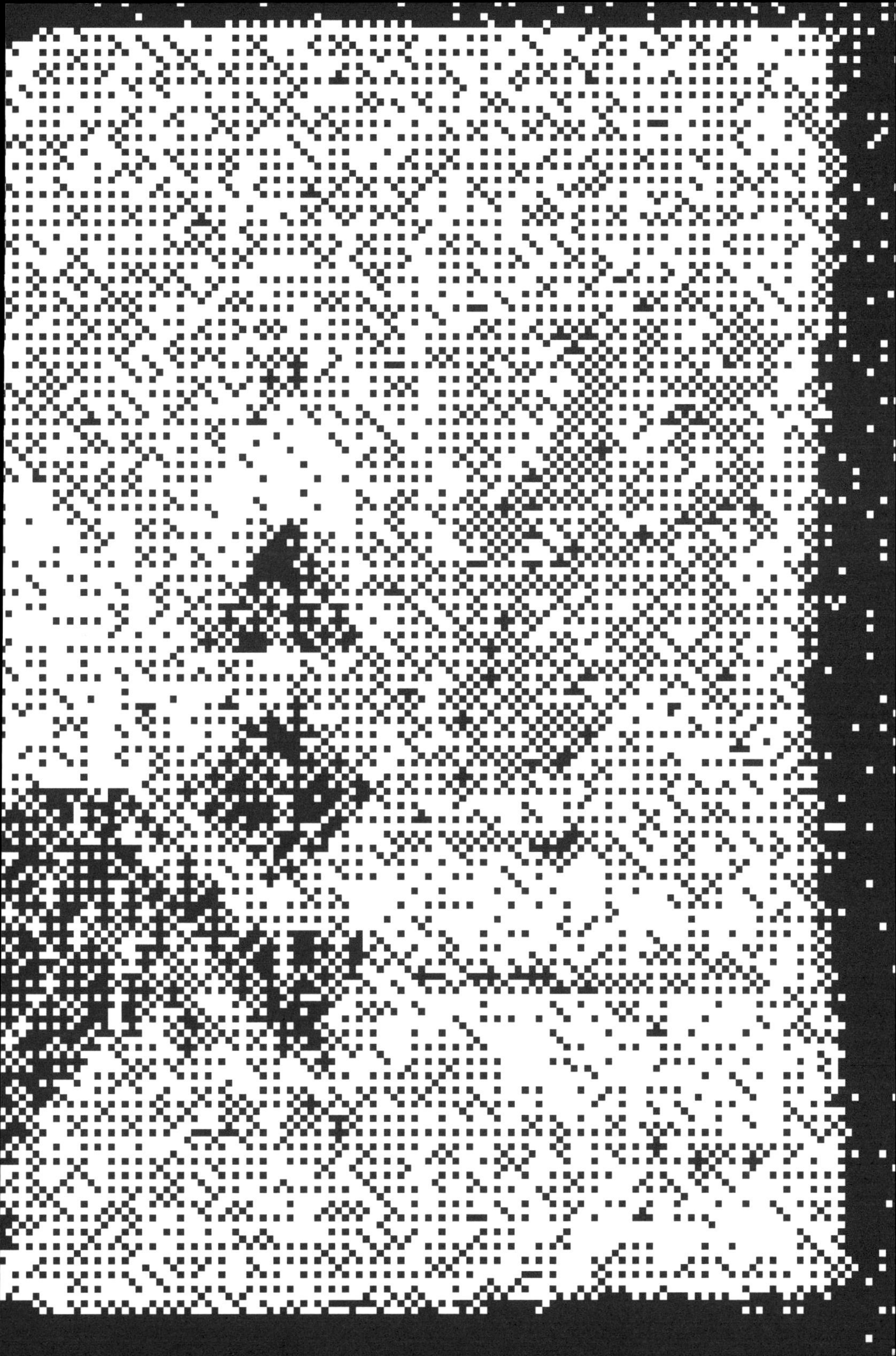

BRITTL

INNO
CHIZAI

PAPER

CENT
AM ILO

Brittle Paper

Innocent Chizaram Ilo

Two ceramic bowls beckon to people as they walk past the Storyteller's shop. From the tiny booth across the street, where Mama Ify sells moi-moi, you can see dimple-faced children painted on the bowls waving at you to come play with them. If you press your ear against the window panes, you will hear the children singing:

    Biakenu, where is it you come from?

    Does your mother's soup rumble in your stomach?

As the dimple-faced children yodel Selemku town awake, the Storyteller's shop begins to come alive. Charcoal sketches of ice-breathing dragons, talons encircled around chicks, people wearing skeletons atop their skins, figures without torsos, their necks connected to their hips, hang from peeling walls. Frayed bristles, upset paint, blank and muddled canvases are strewn over the floor. Balls of wool, a lone thimble, five rusty crochet hooks and a box of knitting pins wrestle in a basket on a mahogany table with termite-punctured holes along its edges.

I

The kettle spurts clouds of crumpled cotton and the stove licks it up in a sizzle and a half as the Storyteller shuffles into the shop from the adjoining cubicle, his bedroom. He lifts the kettle off the stove and pours the boiling water onto a coffee strainer. He smiles as he takes his first sip of coffee from the cup. This has never made sense to him, drinking coffee from a teacup. Wednesday last week, a customer accosted him for using 'coffee cup' instead of 'teacup' in a story.

'Nobody says coffee cup', the woman with a half-burnt face had told him. 'This story is for Little Dodo's birthday party and I swear, you will not ruin it.'

'But he needs to understand you can't drink coffee from a cup and call it a *teacup*.'

'He is only three, why bother him with all that talk?' The woman burst into tears. 'You don't understand, Little Dodo is a special boy. I had him the same day my husband's mistress set our house on fire. Don't you have sympathy for the scars on my face?'

He agreed to the woman's request to change the word just before her tears began to flood the shop. A generous dab of ohs, ahs and 'I'm sorry to hear that' later, the woman sniffed back her remaining tears and hugged the Storyteller until his spine cracked.

'So much for teacups.' He takes another sip and toys with the idea of using her story for another customer. He could twist the plotline, turn the mistress into a dragon-lady... *A storyteller who uses other people's stories, is that a real storyteller?*

The Storyteller walks over to the window and hangs up the 'We Are Open' sign. He settles into a chair, unfolds a blank canvas, and stares at it, as if searching for something – something only he can see. The lines of his jaw constrict into a moue. He starts to paint...

A boy emerges from the curve of the Storyteller's right wrist. He uses brown and a tint of gold for the boy's face. Surreal, and too distorted to decipher who the subject really is. Blue for his singlet and shorts. Moccasin for the dust spiraling around his feet. Red for the two crows perched on an icheku tree.

The Storyteller looks at the canvas and sighs. He should not be painting when he has stories to write.

'Is anyone in?' A voice from outside barges into his thoughts.

The door opens and a gangly man with a lopsided gait walks in. He taps his stick toward the Storyteller and, like all men who have enough coins in their pockets to jingle, offers himself a seat.

'Good morning, Mr Ojinta.'

'Good morning, Mister…?'

'You can call me the Storyteller like everyone else, Mr Ojinta.'

'It still feels strange in my mouth. What kind of man goes by such a name?'

'A man who loves his job.'

'You should have learnt from your master, Odili. Now that's a solid name.'

'What brings you to my shop? Do you want to request a story this time?'

'I wish I had time for that', Mr Ojinta scoffs. 'Have you considered my offer yet?' He is wearing a big grin as he studies the Storyteller's face. 'What if I up my offer by a couple thousand buzas?'

'And why would you do that? It's a small shop, it doesn't even seem worth that much.'

'I see potential and I hate seeing a good space go to waste.'

The Storyteller folds his arms around his chest. 'My business is thriving, Mr Ojinta. This place is not going to waste.'

'For how long will people care about buying stories? I see everything that happens in this town and I see how people no longer troop into the shop like they did when Odili was here. Your customers have reduced to trickles and sometimes days go by with no one coming in at all. Think about it, my good man.'

The Storyteller goes back to staring at his canvas long after the sound of Mr Ojinta's walking stick on the sidewalk has faded. He cannot stand that man. Hates him more now because he knows he is speaking the truth. In the ten years since Odili died and the shop became his, the storytelling business has declined. Maybe, he has told himself time and time again, the people of Selemku simply loved Odili – who wouldn't love Odili, with his punchy jokes and vivacity? Odili's name stuck and was impossible to forget. People found 'the Storyteller', meanwhile, a bland and self-conceited name. They never understood his insistence on being called 'The Storyteller'. *You must have another name, a birth name?* The shop only survived because people still associated it with his predecessor and no one else within a thousand distance sold stories.

Noon. Two customers pop into the shop. The first, Ms Nkoli, a middle-aged woman with a perpetual runny nose, wants a feel-good story for her father, who has been desolate since the death of his second wife. She specifies there should be no mention of her mother, his first wife, in the story. The second drop-in, Deredu, a university professor, wants a cli-fi novella to read from at his daughter's wedding ceremony. Something that will make it clear to guests that he believes his daughter deserves better.

The Storyteller scribbles the story drafts on tracing paper first, before embroidering the words on a piece of muslin. His fingers move with a mind of their own as he sews the letters into the cloth. The Storyteller uses different colors of wool for different words. White for *chapel*, *baby* and *bare*. Blue for *sky*, *lake* and *serene*. Red for *fire*, *fury* and *fear*. Green for *life*, *hope* and *tomorrow*. Yellow for *sun*, *sick* and *tired*. Black for *beauty*, *power* and *storm*.

On his first day as Odili's apprentice, he had asked him why they had to go to the trouble of embroidering words on muslin when they could more efficiently give customers stories on paper. Odili had paused his handwork for a moment to reply: 'Because, sometimes, paper can be too brittle to carry the weight of stories we tell.'

The sun has deepened into the purpling horizon by the time the Storyteller finishes embroidering the stories. He lights an oil lamp and lays out the painting he was working on that morning. The twitching in his fingers rings clear. *Stop – you can't do both*. He ignores the inner warning and unfolds the canvas.

He finishes the sky, taking his time to accentuate the blue-black cloudiness – a readiness to burst open with new rains. He paints a cat, curled around a lightning protector before a brown-zinc bungalow. The boy in the picture knows the cat. Some stray he used to sneak food to, because his mother chased the poor thing away and would not let it eat off their garbage. The brush slips out of his quivering fingers as the form of another child emerges in the middle of the canvas.

See? Too revealing.
There is a knock on the door.
'Who is that?'
'Nnolum, open. It's me.'

The Storyteller knows there is only one person in the world who calls him 'Nnolum'. He opens the door. 'Tochi', the Storyteller greets the man standing in the doorway. The dimming oil lamp casts a shadow on his face. 'Nnua, welcome. How was your journey?'

'It was lovely.'

'You didn't tell me you were coming.' The Storyteller relieves the duffel bag from Tochi's shoulder. 'Ehn? I would have cooked ji awayi for you.' His voice edges toward franticness as he guides him into the shop and locks the door.

'So now I need permission to visit, okwai?' Tochi asks with mock laughter as he pulls the Storyteller closer to him. 'I've missed you, Nnolum.' He cradles the Storyteller's head in his palms and kisses him. The kiss lingers until the Storyteller breaks away to catch his breath. He sets the oil lamp on a stool and blows out the flame.

'I've missed you too.'

The Storyteller unbuttons Tochi's shirt. He nibbles on his lover's neck with the efficiency of one who has done this so much to this body he does not even need light to know the places he will tease to elicit a moan, a sigh, quickened breaths, a hoarse whisper… Tochi unbuckles the Storyteller's belt. The pair of flannels drops to the floor in a whooshing heap.

In one sweep, the Storyteller clears the mahogany table and lays Tochi on it. He parts Tochi's legs and nests his head between them. In turn, Tochi buries his fingers into the Storyteller's hair to steady himself.

'Now, Nnolum, now.'

Tochi pulls the Storyteller up against the counter and guides him inside him.

II

Something about the livened voices emanating from the Storyteller's shop feels off to Zanda. He has been delivering supplies there for months and has never heard anything above a whisper. He peeps through the window to see the Storyteller sitting with a man beside the wooden counter. The man does not look like he is from around here, certainly not with his sunflower cardigan and dreadlocks. His head is tilted at a coy angle as he laughs, flashing a full set of white teeth. He smoothens a crease from his cardigan and pats his hair.

Zanda knocks on the door.

'Who goes there?'

'It's Zanda, Pa Kelechi's son.'

'Oh, Zanda. Come in.'

'Good morning, Storyteller.' Zanda turns to the man: 'Good

morning Sah.'

'You Selemku people and your Sah and Ma. Call me Tochi', Tochi says.

'Okay, Sah.' Zanda opens his tinker box and lays out the supplies on the counter. Five rolls of muslin, wool spools, a crochet and a paint pallet.

Zanda nods. 'My father says he will prepare an invoice later next week and send it over to you.'

The boy turns to leave.

'Are you not going to introduce me to Zanda? Don't be such a terrible host.'

'Well, Zanda. This is Tochi, my… friend. He came all the way from Sua to see me.'

Tochi coughs when the Storyteller says *friend*.

'You're welcome to Selemku, Sah – sorry – Tochi.'

'Ah, thank you, but I am not a stranger. I used to live here.'

'In that case, welcome back.'

'This is Tochi, my… *friend*,' Tochi says as the door closes behind Zanda. 'You know, sometimes I just wish I could throw you away. Do you lay all your friends on that table and fuck them, gbo Nnolum?'

'Can we not start this again?'

'Nnolum, we're not twelve anymore. I'm tired of all this sneaking and hiding and cryptic nonsense.'

'Tochi, stop. You know Selemku is not like Sua. You know how they see people like us. You know people will stop coming to the shop once they know I am…'

'That you're what, Nnolum? You can't even say it. I thought storytellers are supposed to not be afraid of words?'

'Tochi…'

'Please don't Tochi me. If Selemku is not safe, then come to Sua with me.'

'You know how I feel about this place, the shop.'

'You should start asking yourself how this place feels about you, Nnolum.'

The Storyteller starts to put the new supplies away in the basket. 'Maybe you shouldn't have left me here alone.'

'Don't you dare rewrite this story. You were the one who got cold feet the moment Odili chose you to become his apprentice. All of a sudden you wanted to stay back. You started to fall in love with the place that had spit you out.'

'I wanted us to build something together here.'

'And live the rest of my life with my heart in my mouth?'

They eat breakfast in silence, each man seeking comfort in the room's stillness and the warmth of coffee drunk from a teacup.

'Do you want to see the Hall of Fame?' the Storyteller asks after breakfast.

'Sure.'

Tochi nods, trying hard to feign interest. Nnolum has shown him the gallery behind the bookshelf with pictures of all the past storytellers each time he has visited.

The Storyteller leads the way.

'Who is this?' Tochi points at the first picture in the topmost row. 'I love his black beret.'

'That's Beche. Have you forgotten? He was the one who started this shop.'

Tochi's eyes roam around the pictures, picking up on distinctive features – Sole's snow-white hair; Gugi's smile that makes his cheeks look like carelessly drawn commas; Mpa's plastic-framed glasses; Uchi's cornrows that spring out of her Ankara headwrap; Lechi's unruffled face, which makes Tochi wonder what was going on in his mind; Essie's remarkable pose, her chin pushed forward with her balled right fist; Laye's lips parted like someone who is not done telling a story; Odili's hair dyed like a popstar's.

The Storyteller waits for Tochi to retire for the night before he brings out the painting. He completes the figure of the other boy on a new canvas. The two boys are now holding hands on a dusty path that stops before a hedge of wilted marigolds. He knows that, in reality, the flowers had just blossomed. But who else would know? The hedge borders a house with white walls. He smudges the wall with brown paint because he can remember rubbing his muddied palms on it, all those years ago.

The Storyteller dozes off on his chair with the paintbrush between the loose grip of his fingers.

III

A stray dog yapping at a beggar on the street wakes the Storyteller up. His right arm is sore from having been slept on. He smiles as the clatter of pots and pans filters into the room. Tochi is already up and the kettle is boiling on the stove. The Storyteller watches as Tochi hangs up the 'We Are Open' sign, his eyes following him as he sets the table for breakfast.

'Words are magical. I think that is why I love doing this.' The Storyteller dips a biscuit into his coffee. 'You see three random letters: A, N, T. But when you put them together, they become a tiny crawling thing.' He does not think Tochi is listening but continues anyway. 'And in that tiny ant, there is a story. Is it brown like cowpea pods? Does it crawl over a lump of sugar?'

They have barely finished breakfast before three customers walk into the shop. Ms Agbodike and Oearl are here to ask if the Storyteller is done with their stories. Uzu, the blacksmith, wants a story-rewrite because the one he collected a week ago slipped into his forging furnace.

'Uzu, how many times will I tell you that muslin does not agree with fire?'

Rewriting stories scares him. Like revisiting a ghost. But his contract obligates him to offer a three-month warranty for every story he sells.

'The story was too good. I wanted to show it off to my fellow blacksmiths', Uzu replies.

'I will rewrite it but you have to promise me you will never take it to work with you.'

Uzu chews at his tongue.

'You are going to take it to work, aren't you?'

Night creeps in like a thief. The Storyteller waits for Tochi's deep snoring to drown the chirping of the crickets before he brings out the painting. On another canvas, he paints a man and a woman standing beside a house. The woman's powdered face is caked because she has been crying and the man is fire-red with fury. How his parents had stood in front of their house the day they caught him and Tochi kissing behind the hedge.

What is he going to do with the painting – continue? Where will this story end? With his parents' marriage unraveling at the seams as they accuse each other of making him the way he is? Then dying once they run out of accusations? Or with the dreams of leaving he nursed with Tochi, until Odili took him in? There is a version of this story where they depart to live in Sua and spend their evenings holding hands and blowing bubbles into the wind. There is a version of this story where nothing happens: no house with the marigold hedge, no Tochi, no him – just emptiness.

The Storyteller squeezes the canvas and tosses it into the fireplace. Goosebumps crawl along his skin as the waning, yellow fangs reduce it to ash. A raspy voice echoes, You don't do that, Nnolum. You don't go around kissing your fellow boy behind the flower hedge. It's a sin. It's a sin. Sin. Sin lures him to sleep.

IV

'Wake up, Nnolum. Your skin is molting.'

The Storyteller opens his eyes. 'What time is it?'

'It's been morning for a while now. Why are your bones jutting out of your skin, Nnolum? What is happening to you? Should I send for a doctor? I should send for a doctor.'

'Stop panicking, Tochi. I think I have Hiatus.'

'Hiatus?'

'Some kind of periodic ailment that afflicts storytellers when they exhaust all the stories inside them.'

Tochi is not reassured. 'How long until it stops?'

'I don't know. Probably a day or two.'

It's the first time the Storyteller has suffered from Hiatus. Odili always told him this day would come – he has been expecting it for the past twenty years. Some storytellers cured Hiatus by soaking themselves in a muse-potion made by boiling some of a storyteller's writing drafts in water. Others simply waited it out.

This Storyteller comes down with a fever after Tochi has soaked him in the muse-potion. Tochi helps him attend to the customers, taking down their requests and apologizing to the ones for whom the Storyteller could not complete their story at present. In the evening, the fever worsens. The Storyteller's eyes are red-red and his lips look like they are packed with concrete. He groans from the pain of his bones scraping against the bed frame.

Tochi sits by his side and sings him to sleep.

The fever has died down and his skin has stopped molting when he wakes up later.

    'How are you now?' asks Tochi.

    'Better. I think it doesn't have a hold on me any longer.'

    'Do you want to eat anything?'

    'No.' He gets up to open the window. 'I just want to gaze at the sky. The moon is full tonight.'

    Tochi clears his throat. 'Come with me to Sua, Nnolum. You'll like it there. We could hold hands in the streets and no one would spit at us. You can start your story business there and you can write about people like us, men who fall in love with other men. Don't you think stories like ours deserve to be embroidered on fancy muslin?'

    'But what about this shop? What about my customers?'

    'The same people who would shove you into the gutter if they knew who you really are?' Tochi scoffs. 'I'm not asking you to make a decision now. I'm not asking you to come to Sua tomorrow.'

    The Storyteller reaches out for Tochi to kiss him. 'Maybe, just maybe, one day I will come to Sua with you.'

    'Goodnight, Nnolum.'

The dimple-faced children do not sing today. When you ask them about the water gathering in their eyes, they swear it's dewdrops. In the dewdrops lie the promises lovers make in locked embraces before departures. One man leaves with the fear that one day he will grow tired of prodding the other, that one day he will stop asking his lover to come away with him, and that one day he will leave and never come back. The other unfolds a new canvas. Perhaps this time, the boy in the painting will make him remember what it feels like to be free.

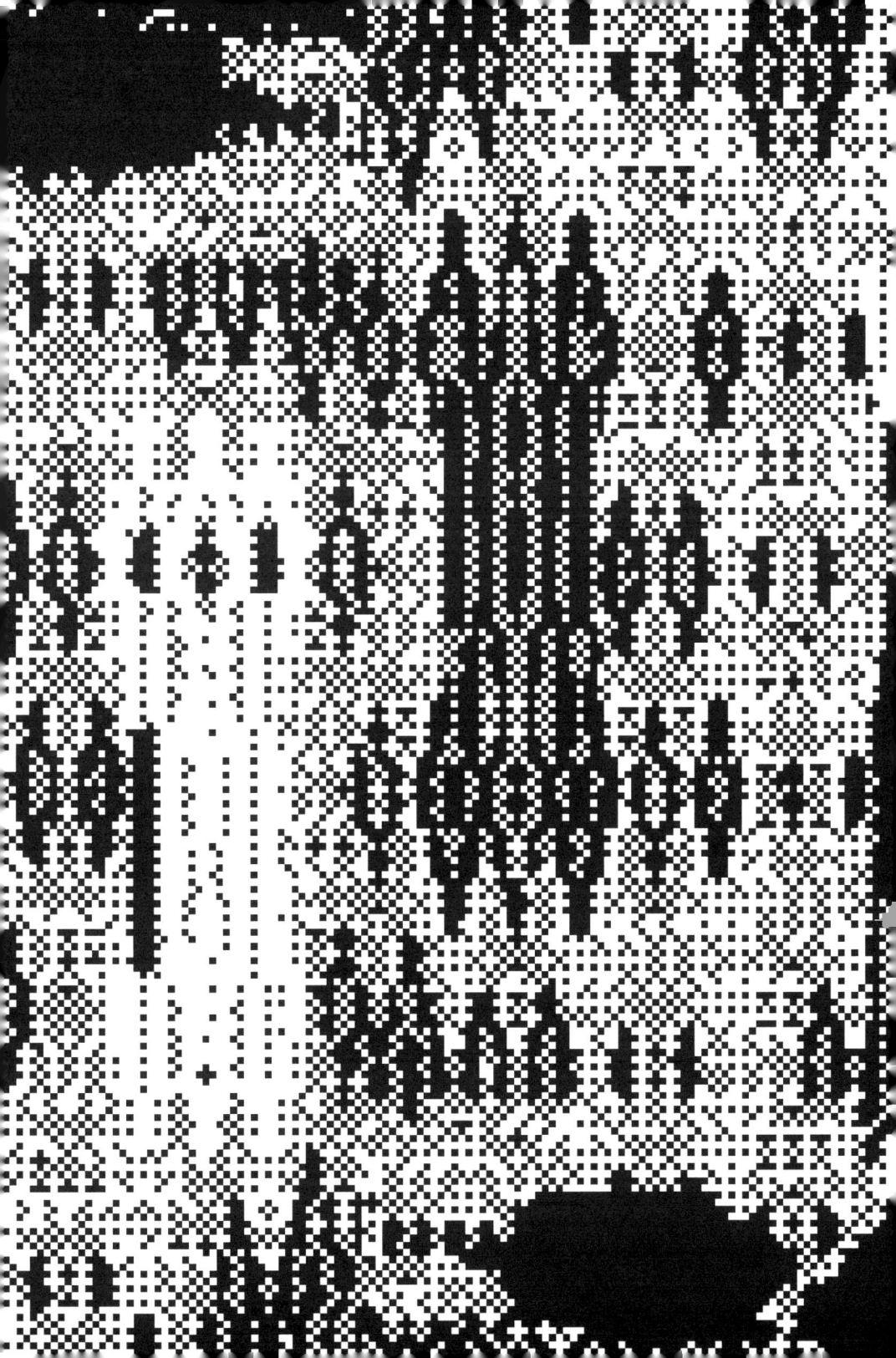

MOR
RION A
SC

More Life

Rion Amilcar Scott

My father's dead eyes had always stared back at me for as long as I'd had memory, from my days as a young guy well into adulthood. Life took something from Dad and it kept taking every day, until shortly after he moved in with me and he sat on that chair in the living room to watch a night of television and expired right there. I didn't at first recognize his dead eyes as truly dead. It annoyed me that he'd left the television on all night while he slept, but when I saw his open eyes, I was seized by another annoyance.

    Dad, you have to actually go to bed sometimes, I said from across the room.

    When that yielded no response, yet another layer of irritation washed over me. Dad didn't respond to statements or people he thought beneath him, and I often found myself on the wrong side of his silence—less since becoming an adult, but still sometimes he said nothing when I spoke. He grew tired of me telling him he needed to repair his sleep habits. I knew what I was speaking about. His lack of sleep did such violence to his memory, and his tremors needed rest if they were to ever disappear.

    One way to turn me monstrous, everyone knew, was to ignore me. I had no more sensitive trigger than disregard, so many relationships of all sorts fell to pieces under the heat of my shouting after someone had made me invisible. I still drove by the home of a woman whom I love, but who blocked me online after a shouting match. Just evaporated me quickly, as if we hadn't both promised that our connection would be forever. I've grown better over time, learned to simply walk away, to linger in and even enjoy incorporeality, but no one triggered me quite like my father. The rage beast began rising through my blood. I was preparing, despite knowing better, to give it to him.

    Dad, I said sharply, I told you about getting to bed at a decent time. It's—

    I drew closer to the chair and my motionless father. He never sat entirely motionless, nowadays; tremors forever shook him against his will.

Now, his face had masked up, that's how I knew he was dead. I touched his cheek. A human wasn't supposed to be this cold. Perhaps he had already passed when I said good night and kissed that same cheek just hours ago, warning him to go to bed after the football game ended. He said nothing back, but figuring that the men in helmets and pads mattered most to him in the moment, I didn't let that particular snubbing move me in any way.

Remembering his eyes from the night before did nothing to tell me if he was already dead when I had left. Now, the rest of him joined those deceased pupils in the great beyond.

I slumped to my father's side and gripped his cold left hand. What was I supposed to do? I had no idea. Call 911? But this wasn't an emergency. The emergency had happened hours ago. Nothing could be done to help him rejoin the living. The impossibility of the next few weeks, or months, passed over me as a shudder—so much business to conduct that would make no sense to me, and no siblings to help, just me. Never, since my childhood days when I wanted a playmate, did I resent being an only child more than I did at the moment. My stomach cried for something to fill it. My dead father would have to wait until after I'd eaten.

Want an omelet, Pop?

Yes, he said in a whisper, barely moving his lips.

I jumped back, startled. He turned his head slightly, then just sat there, still dead. I knew what I saw, but I remained unable to trust my mind. I touched his cheek, the chill of a harsh winter along his flesh.

Dad, I said to no response. I stood there for a good ten minutes, listening and feeling for breath, looking for any sign of life returning—but nothing. I must have called his name twenty times, but he didn't move. I had to regard that moment of brief life as a hallucination. But you know what I did when I went to the kitchen? Like a clownish chef, I prepared an omelet, sausages and coffee for him too, just in case.

At eight o'clock sharp, I finished with my meal and was tossing my father's—I had left it on a tray in front of him and the ungrateful fool hadn't touched it—when my phone rang. A mousy, distant voice squeaked into my ear:

Hello? I'm looking for a Mr Andrew Chalet.

I'm sorry, Andrew Chalet is my father and he's... he's... um... he's unavailable now, may I ask who is calling?

Oh, I'm sorry, I got the names mixed up here, I'm looking for Jerome Chalet.

This is he, I said. A burning annoyance had started building inside me, and I tried to convey it to the caller by sharpening my tone. May I ask—

First of all, I'm sorry for your loss. According to our records, Mr Andrew Chalet has passed, am I correct?

I, um—Just who am I speaking with now?

I'm sorry, Mr Chalet. This is never, ever an easy call. My name is Howard Mason, and I'm with Vivid Life: Has your father mentioned us to you?

No. What is *Vivid Life*, and how do you know that my father has passed? I'd appreciate if you'd cut to the chase. He's only been dead for a few hours, and I haven't informed any—

Yes. Yes, and I'm sorry. We would have called earlier, only he passed in the overnight hours and we don't have any Monitors currently working at that time, especially not on a Friday night. I've been lobbying for more funding to have people here so we can avoid situations like this, but—this is so much inside baseball. Your father was gracious enough to trust us to include him in a pretty unprecedented study. We tell participants to alert their families but that is not always honored. We've had to make many calls like this. I'll send along the paperwork, but part of being in this study means that his body goes to Vivid Life upon expiration.

I still don't understand how you knew—

Ah yes, the big questions. So, there is a mapping device we placed in your father's head. It serves a double function. It helped calm your father's Parkinson's tremors—

My father had Parkinson's?

Yes. Many of our participants have ailments that affect memory, cognition, and in your father's case, mobility and control of the body. The device also creates a second-by-second map of all the brain's processes. This study is the most exciting thing I've ever been a part of, and your father agreed. I told him we couldn't cure him, but we'd learn more about the brain's functions in a couple months than we have in all of history. Your dad seemed really in awe of that. The other exciting thing is that we essentially have a backup of your father here in our computer systems.

Sorry, what?

These calls have gotten so frequent that they have tended to be quite impersonal, which I regret. We've started inviting family members to take a tour so they know what their loved ones have signed up for and can be comfortable with us being in possession of their loved ones' bodies. Would that appeal to you?

Uh, a tour? When?

As soon as possible. When our people come to pick up your dad you can ride here with them. I'll be dispatching them after we finish this call. If you check your email, I have sent all our paperwork and attached a pamphlet on what Vivid Life does.

I felt numb after I set down the phone. I paced around the house and stared out the window. How could my father never mention something like this? When I looked at him again, it almost appeared like he was trying to stir. But I knew it to be my mind's trickery. Eventually, I looked over the paperwork Howard Mason had sent me. Yep, those were my father's signatures. Mason even sent me a video of my father speaking: I, Andrew Chalet, am of sound mind and would like to turn over my body to Vivid Life for further study upon my passing.

Well, if this is what he wanted, I thought.

The Vivid Life pamphlet was full of blue skies and smiling people. On the front it read: *Vivid Life: A Meratti Company*. Meratti sold much of the medical equipment the business I work for distributed. Even the fork I ate breakfast with came out of a box stamped with a Meratti logo. I felt a bit better knowing that this company, Vivid Life, wasn't just some fly-by-night but part of a company I trusted. Their slogan was simple but effective: *More Life*. They were working to reveal the hidden secrets of the brain, they said. They were using *cutting-edge technology* and *state-of-the-art systems and processes*. It all seemed so vague, yet also intriguing.

I wanted to tell my old love, Mimi, about all this. Wanted to receive her comfort for the loss of my dad. Wanted to say, You're not going to believe this... I raised my phone to text her, before remembering that not a text, call, email or social media message from me could reach her in my current state of non-existence.

Well, Dad, I said, patting his shoulder. I don't know what you got us into, boy.

I thought I heard him turn and grunt—but no, he was settled, unmoving. I passed my hand over the sharp tips of my closely cropped hair. Losing my father, I thought, so suddenly and so strangely, would render me insane.

It took several hours for the people from Vivid Life to arrive. Two of them—one tall and solid, one shorter and heavy-set—stepped out of a long white van with the name of the company in sky-blue letters and a picture of the brain floating between the two words. I opened the door and greeted them, but they didn't return my hellos. They grunted and walked past me, with tablets in their hands, and found my father in his chair.

The men were dressed oddly in what looked like rubber aprons and sleek football helmets. A white plastic mask covered the nose and mouth so all you could see of their faces were eyes that appeared red and black, with popped blood vessels and not a blessed bead of life.

Mr Chalet, the taller one said in a low whisper. He held out a tablet to me. A box on the screen indicated that I was to sign. While I read the form, some kind of a waiver, the stocky man went back outside and returned with a black body bag.

The tall Vivid Life guy touched my father's shoulder with a gloved hand. I thought my insanity was acting up again, as I swore I saw my father jerk forward and grunt. Then, all two hundred and fifty pounds of him stood and howled in the masked face of the man who had touched him.

Step back, please, the chunky helmeted man said to me in an aggravated whisper. Then he shouted: We have a Lifer!

Just what the hell! I screamed, noticing the cattle prod in his thick left hand. The tall man raised his arms wide above his head, making himself even bigger, as if scaring off a bear, and uttered a low growl while stepping backward. My father walked slowly toward the tall man, while the shorter man approached him from behind with the cattle prod. Just when it seemed that my dead father was about to lunge at the first man, the other man placed the prod at the base of my father's skull. I gasped as an electric buzz sounded and my father collapsed to the floor.

I stood staring down at him and at the men who were now hovering over his body. The man who had zapped him reached into the pocket of his apron and handed me another pamphlet with *Vivid Life* at the top. Beneath the logo it read: *What Does It Mean When the Dead Come Back?*

Man. What the fuck is happening? You're going to have to explain this to me right now! At that moment all our phones began to buzz, and the Vivid Lifers stepped outside to answer their calls.

You're just going to walk away from me? Leave my dad on the—

They were already gone, ignoring me as if I were a ghost to them. I would have followed the men raging, but my phone needed my attention.

Hello?

The mousy voice again.

Jerome. Howard Mason from Vivid Life here. Some of the Monitors alerted me to a surge. Looks like your dad is a Lifer!

A what?

Many exciting and unexpected things have happened with this study. Frankly, I'm floored. We have no idea where life ends and death starts. None. Look, there is more I need to explain to you and I can't do it over the phone. The guys have to do a few extra things to make sure your father transports well, since he's a Lifer and all, so don't worry about riding with them. I'll send a car and we can talk and I can give you that tour. I realize we haven't made a great impression and I want you to be comfortable that your father is in good hands. How's that sound?

I stood outside waiting for the car as the men worked inside, doing God knows what to my father's living yet still dead corpse. The driver that pulled up wore dark sunglasses, a chauffeur's cap and a slack-jawed expression. He grunted and waved me to the backseat. All I could think of as we drove was my father. I remembered when I had noticed those tremors, not long after Mom died. I started going over to keep him company at dinner time some nights, and he kept clinking the fork against the plate.

It's nothing, he had said when I asked. Sometimes grief is physical, you know.

He mentioned some doctor's appointments but said nothing of Parkinson's.

They told me to keep active, he said. That'll make the shakies go away. I'm working with a physical therapist.

I thought it was strange for him to be prescribed physical therapy as a remedy for an ailment without physical origins, but didn't think much of it. He told me he'd be taking leave from his plumbing job, which was mostly installing water heaters these days. Wasn't feasible in his state. Just a temporary thing.

He never returned to his work. Soon after leaving his job, he started going to a boxing class for seniors at a rec center near my place. When the tremors didn't cease, I invited him to join me for a jog in the park next to the center a few times. He trailed me, almost leisurely. If this is how he does those classes, I thought, no wonder the tremors had only gotten worse. My father, I figured, needed a drill sergeant, not a panderer. The second time we went out, I jogged ahead, stopped about ten yards in front of him and shouted:

Gotta put more speed on that, old man. Come on.

I gave him a gentle shove as he passed.

Keep up, Pop, you got it!

I repeated this a couple more times until my father exploded: I'm not training for the goddamn Olympics, 'Rome. Fuck this, take me home!

My father ignored me the whole way back to his apartment, gazing out the car window at the passing world. When we got to the parking lot, he turned to me, but I opened my mouth to speak first.

Remember when I used to play basketball, I asked, soccer, and all that stuff, and you used to stand on the side encouraging me, wouldn't let me settle for not making an effort?

What is this, revenge?

Nooo. You taught me important lessons, jack. I just want to help you make the tremors stop.

Encouraging you? You think you felt encouraged? Remember your mother stopped coming to the games, especially when I started coaching. You remember that? She said I was making a damn fool of myself and hurting you. I was probably the age you are now. Looking at you in the park is like looking back in time into a very ugly mirror.

No wonder Mimi left you, he said, before slamming the car door.

I watched my father walk up to the apartment that remained a shrine to my mom, fighting the urge to trot behind him and yank him to the ground. When he entered his home, I knew he'd forget me; it was a place of peace for him. Pop had made not a single change in decor in the two years and some months since my mother had passed. He even kept those Mickey Mouse tchotchkes she cluttered the place with. How many hours of our lives had he spent mocking those figurines, never missing the chance to tell my mother he hated them, never letting up when the evil spirit hit him? Mom would suppress her annoyance for a while to keep the peace, but eventually she would rage. Now it seemed the Mickey Mouses didn't bother him; they even comforted him.

My father and I never apologized to each other or talked about our disagreements—that simply wasn't our way. We just ignored one another for a while and then I'd call him, or more often, he'd call me, or I'd show up at his place to cook a meal. We didn't work out together after that, though. The tremors became like another person in our relationship, one we rarely acknowledged but who still shaped all our interactions.

When I arrived at the Vivid Life offices, Howard Mason stood outside. He opened the car door and when I stepped out, he tightly embraced me as if we were old friends. Howard tapped the car's trunk and the driver grunted and pulled off.

My apologies again for this morning, he said. This is not the impression we'd like to make.

Look, I saw my dead dad come to life, and then I saw your employees kill him again—

Oh, he didn't come to life per se, and our people didn't *kill* him. Come, let's walk. We entered the building and strode to the elevator. Howard waved a card over a reader and we shot up to the eleventh floor. He was trying to explain the mechanics of what was happening with my father, but I couldn't follow. As we stepped out of the elevator and walked to the office, I replayed the argument that brought my dad to live with me:

If you fall again, and you don't make it—what am I supposed to do then?

Tears beaded in his eyes and I knew I had properly guilted him into moving in.

When we got to Howard's office, I sat across from him and he offered me coffee or tea. I declined.

Howard, I don't get any of this, I said.

Neither do we, 'Rome—that's what your dad calls you, right? I saw that on the screen when reviewing your father's brain map.

Jerome is fine.

The mapping device is supposed to read all the electricity flowing through the brain and build a map of the tangible flow of consciousness, Howard explained. And it works so much better than we expected. At the moment of death, there is a surge of electricity in the brain; what no one could have anticipated is that after that surge, consciousness continues in a diminished form. For some of our subjects, the brain attempts to use the signals the mapping device has collected to return life to the body. We call those people Lifers. This manifests in its crudest form as what you witnessed with your father, but we've been working to offer some control over the return-to-life process.

What do you mean?

Those guys who collected your dad, your driver?

You're saying—

Yep, dead.

I leaned back in my seat trying to formulate some coherent words, but all I could think of was the dirty, blood-clot-ridden eyes of the helmeted men and the driver's slack jaw.

Howard, you're—I don't—you're rearranging my understanding of—I'm not sure this is the place I want to leave my—

That so many of our subjects don't talk this over with their families has been a bit of a thorn in our sides, 'Rome. I'm in it for the science, not the confrontations. The business part is a necessary evil. A lot of businesses are going to spin off of our findings. Some already have. Our legal department is top-notch. The agreements we have our subjects sign are air-tight. Still, we've already had families take us to court and other nonsense. It's just a waste of everyone's time. I think in the future we'll make sure to involve family, but I haven't made that a prio— There I go again, prattling on. Andrew, could you come in here, please?

The door opened and in walked a bot, humanoid in shape. All white, with an unmoving mannequin face. No clothes or genitals.

'Rome, you're wearing that stupid-looking blue shirt again, the bot said. I think I bought that for you when you were, what, ten?

My dad loved this dumb joke. He had bought the shirt for me, not when I was ten, but about ten years ago. He made fun of me the first time I wore it. I think he bought it for me just to mock me. It really didn't fit anymore. I don't know why I still wear it. The mannequin, although blank-looking, had my father's voice.

Howard, I said. I—What—

Howard walked behind the bot and tapped its head three times. I saw the bot freeze and the light leave its face. He pulled a small cylinder from the back of the bot's head.

This, 'Rome, he said, as he held the cylinder in the palm of his hand, is your father. It only takes about a week of mapping to create an Independent Living Consciousness and imprint it into one of these little Consciousness Cylinders. We've been mapping your dad for a year. And that death surge is very helpful.

That's the thing you had in my dad's brain?

No, of course not. The mapping device is a tiny chip. Takes less than thirty minutes to install. No cutting necessary. We leave it in there until... well, let's just say it's still there.

Howard walked behind the bot and patted its shoulder. The thing jerked forward and I was afraid it would topple, but it didn't.

This mannequin-like figure here is a ReVivid, Howard said. This is a three-month model, so after that time it will be nonfunctional. It'll only take us about two months to fabricate a bio-mechanical Permabody to place your father's consciousness in. It'll look just like him. Move just like him, save for the tremors. Or we can program those in, if you'd like. It'll be him, 'Rome, if you want it. We've hacked grief. Disrupted death. That stuff isn't necessary anymore. In the future, this will be worth hundreds of thousands, but you can have your father back for free. If you'll just sign some forms promising you won't tie us up in court with some frivolous lawsuit over your dad's body.

I thought about what Howard was saying, until the silence of the moment sat atop us like a heavy weight.

So what happens to my dad?

Your dad is right here.

Howard opened his palm again to show me the cylinder.

After you sign off on all this, we'll remove your dad's consciousness from our systems so that it will only be available to you. The body is just a meat-frame. We'll do further study on it and, as I said, the businesspeople will figure out monetization.

So my dad will be, what, collecting bodies and chauffeuring people around?

A good portion of our funding comes from our monetization efforts, 'Rome. Renting out Lifers. Saving on salaries by having Lifers perform appropriate tasks. I don't see your dad collecting bodies or driving, but I'm hoping to get some Lifers to be Monitors so we can have coverage overnight and avoid late notifications like what happened with you. Lifers don't need to sleep. Go ahead and think about it, 'Rome. I'll run out of the room and leave you to have some time with your father.

He slid the cylinder back into the ReVivid's head and its arms began to move. It lifted its head and said: 'Rome?

This is your father, Howard assured me as he walked out the door. The body that was failing him is already gone. We'll get you a new one.

What did I do? What would you have done? We had a glorious two weeks, me and Dad. At first his language came out scrambled sometimes, but it only took a day or two for him to get the hang of his new body and his extended life. He kept saying: They got me in this plastic dummy, huh?

Soon it'll be a new flesh-suit, Pop, I replied one time. We can go out jogging.

Hmm. We'll see. I was only doing that to get rid of the tremors. I don't even have them anymore!

He couldn't remember anything after his death, or the night of it. We laughed about the Vivid Lifers putting him down with a cattle prod. Late at night he'd retire to the chair and watch sports channels or old *Sanford and Son* episodes until dawn.

Pop, I'd tell him, they said you should shut down at night to preserve the ReVivid's shell. If it expires before the new body is ready, the Consciousness Cylinder could burn out without a home.

Bah, let me watch my show. Your mother loved this episode, you know. I nagged her about getting enough sleep instead of staying up to watch it with her, and now I can't. Get you an old lady to nag, 'Rome. Then you wouldn't have to worry about nagging your dead father.

The next day, I got another call from Howard to tell me that Dad's body would be ready in a week. When I told Dad, he nodded his mannequin head. I wish he'd had animated facial features so I could see his happiness, or whatever it was he felt. He said:

Son, since I've been back, I haven't seen the river. Let's go at sundown. Let me see the sun go red and blaze over the water like we did when you were young. You know, me and your mother used to do that a lot after you got up out the house. Let me see it with these robot eyes, then I can compare it with whatever robo-flesh eyes they're gonna give me next.

People will stare at us, I said. Me and my mannequin.

Do a favor for an old, dead man, he said.

So we went out to Bimin Promenade as the sun dipped into the river. A few people watched and pointed at us, but no one interrupted as we sat on the wall that separated land from water.

What it look like, Pop?

Like a painting, he said. Almost pixelated, though. Still beautiful.

He waved his hand in front of his face. Laughed a bit. A barge in the distance blew black smoke into the air. A seagull squawked in the sky.

Technology is some crazy shit. Three weeks ago, I was dead. I'm still dead, 'Rome.

Pop, you're as real and alive as you ever been. We got a chance to go to amusement parks we never been to. Fancy dinners. Plays. You never saw the last August Wilson one, right? I got us tickets to see the Commanders for when that body arrives. Road trip, Pop! And we can go to Italy like you always wanted. World without end, Pop.

I'm like a video-game character or something, 'Rome. Call me Mario, like the Nintendo guy. You're right, I'm not dead. But I'm not real either, 'cause I was never alive. I know how to install a water heater, but I've never done it. I remember the night you were conceived, but look at me, I have no genitals. How long they say that Permabody will last?

They're not sure, at least a hundred years.

One hundred years. You think you'll be around a hundred years from now?

Maybe I'll join the study too, get me a Permabody. You know all those arguments we had? The distance, the silent treatment? You yelling at me at my basketball game, me yelling at you while jogging? We can erase all that and replace those bad times with new memories. We can do better, both of us.

No offense, 'Rome. I loved you—just a bit less than I loved your mother—but I don't want to spend eternity with you. I wanted to spend a long life with her, and we did that. Not as long as I wanted. And then life ended me, just like it ended her. Go out and find what me and your mother had. Wasn't perfect, but I enjoyed it. I'm sorry I called you worthless at that basketball game when you were sixteen. You're not worthless. You're no good at basketball, but you're definitely not worthless. I should have apologized in the car that night. I felt like shit and knew I was wrong. I should have said sorry any time it occurred to me since that day. It's amazing how much you can think about and recall when you don't have to worry about losing control of your shaking limbs. That day keeps coming back to me. Other days too. I'm sorry for all of them. And I'm sorry I never really said sorry. I'm not your dad, buddy, though I'm a remarkable simulation of him. He never had the presence of mind to apologize. I can tell you he wanted to; thought about it a lot, but never did. Or maybe I've been programmed to feel that way. I can't say for sure, 'Rome.

I reached for Dad's plastic hand and held it. His fingers felt cold and inanimate, and I thought about how soon they would be soft and warm, an indistinguishable simulation of life; how eventually he'd feel not like a replacement bot but like my true father. After a moment, Dad threw his arms into the air and without another word, slid from the wall into the river.

I screamed for my father as I watched his ReVivid body break apart and sink—with the exception of his head, which turned round and round as it floated on its side in the direction of the fading sun. In this state of shock and helplessness, I considered jumping in and swimming to my father's plastic remains. What stopped me was how the head spun slowly in the water, and that, every time it faced me, I thought I saw a smile creep onto its mannequin lips.

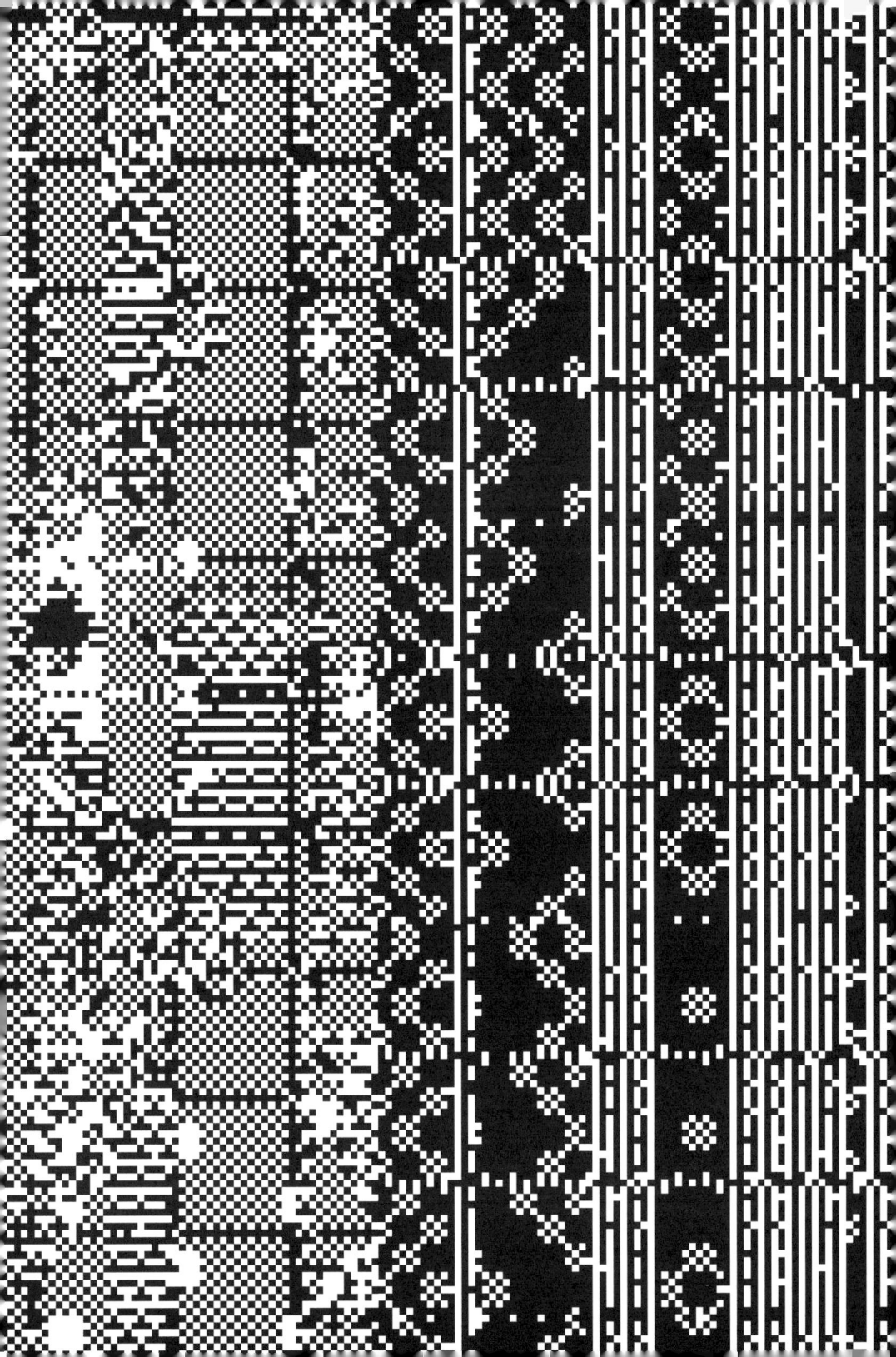

WHEN VIE
THE HEAD
THE
SIMON

VED FROM
THER THAN
OOT

OKOTIE

When Viewed From the Head Rather Than the Foot

Simon Okotie

Yet as she rolled from her left side onto her back by pressing, with her right hand, on the internal rear façade of that eight- or twelve-sided three-dimensional enclosure and, at the moment her centre of gravity passed to the right beyond the base formed by that left side, simultaneously removing that right hand and retracting her right arm, initially by, as it were, folding that arm around its elbow and then, as the hand passed to the right of her torso, unfolding it again around the same joint and revolving it progressively around its shoulder-, elbow- and wrist-joints, such that the hand was in a position to land to her right on the base of that space and act as a shock-absorber for the remainder of her body as the latter revolved, clockwise when viewed from the head rather than the foot, which is to say, when viewed from a position on the superior side of a transverse section through her body, under the force, now, entirely, of gravity, towards a supine position, she found that, rather than being able to adopt a position whereby, through bending her knees, she could place her feet flat such that, by subsequently exerting a force through the soles of those feet, she would be able to raise her torso from that base by arching her back, her feet and shoulders as the 'bridge piers', if that's the correct term, such that she would finally be able to release her left hand which, for now, remained trapped beneath her given it had been behind her when she'd been in that recumbent position on her left side, with this manoeuvre being, in fact, a mere staging post en route to her ultimate objective, which was to move forward within that space, which is to say, to move to her right towards the front of that space given that that eight- or twelve-sided three-dimensional enclosure was conveying her from left to right from her perspective, this being the most likely façade, in her estimation, from which to effect her eventual release therefrom, she found that, instead of her heels moving towards her, which is to say, instead of moving towards her backside such that the angle subtended by the upper and lower legs would progressively decrease in proportion to that decreasing distance, and I could hardly avoid being implicated, she thought, given our multiple mutual entanglements, the equivalent angle between feet and shins increasing accordingly as her toes moved towards the ground or base of that space, remained resolutely in place, which is to say that her heels made no movement, implying that, despite the signal having been sent by her, so far as she could tell, urgently if unthinkingly, in the usual way, for this manoeuvre to commence, which is to say the movement of the heels along their, and her, resting place towards her buttocks, this latter word preferable to her than the previous way in which she'd referred to this three-dimensional region – the 'backside' – in that it was, she thought, both more specifically technical – less colloquial – and more evocative of the fleshy parts of its counterparts, the heels, as well, of course, as being pluralised like those counterparts, which is to say that it evoked and to some extent paralleled the shape and relative fleshiness of the latter, not, of course, that she blamed me exactly, she thought, for her predicament – that wasn't what we were saying – perhaps unsurprisingly given the shock-absorbent function served by both zones or regions, one pair in relation, of course, to standing, walking and (dare she say it) dancing, the other in relation, primarily but perhaps not exclusively, to sitting, that the signal had, somehow, gone unreceived or unrecognised, meaning, in short, that she was literally and metaphorically powerless and in the hands of others, at least, that is, in relation to the lower limbs, the upper being, so far as she could tell, still capable of receiving her volitional transmissions, the right arm, of course, being the one best suited to testing this hypothesis in that it was relatively unencumbered, as it were, by the rest of the body, remaining, as it was, more or less free in its articulations as her right hand approached the base of that enclosure to the right of her torso, meaning that it, at least, was available to assist her in moving in the manner described, which is to say, to assist her in moving towards attaining a position whereby she would be able to release her left hand from beneath her, such that she could use that hand with its counterpart to manipulate further the remainder of her body, through whatever means, in such a way as to adopt a posture within that enclosure whereby she might eventually effect her release therefrom, a strategy and approach that she decisively, now, modified, given not only that her right hand had finally touched down upon the base of that space to the right of her torso, but also that the space itself, as though in response to this additional contact, had started to tilt backwards, consistent, that is, with it having started up a ramp in a forwards direction, such that its leading edge had gained elevation in relation to its trailing edge, with this development being, of course, contrary to her aspiration to move forwards within that space, as though through, as it were, placing her therein, she thought, I had this indirect control over her on its part – given, that is, that her body was arranged laterally within it such that a backwards – or upwards – tilt objectively translated into a leftwards tilt subjectively – thereby opposing, or resisting, the clockwise revolution around her longitudinal axis when viewed from the head rather than the foot, which is to say, when viewed from a position on the superior side of a transverse section through her body, that she had so long aspired to, leaving her wondering why it was that, rather than actively resisting this motion on her part, which is to say, actively resisting the motion induced, or potentially induced, in her by the front of that eight- or twelve-sided three-dimensional space elevating itself consistent with it entering upon an upwards ramp in a forwards direction such that this would induce in her a counter-clockwise revolution around her longitudinal axis which would serve to send her back to the position of resting on her left side from which she had commenced this whole manoeuvre, this resistance taking the form, for instance, of her placing her right hand, which, remember, remained at liberty and available to her, unlike its counterpart, the left, back upon the internal rear façade of that space, and applying an equal and opposite pressure to that being applied upon her by the increasing elevation of the front of that space in relation to its rear, which is to say, the counter-clockwise revolution around the space's rear axle when viewed from the right of that space as it moves from left to right in front of us, this equal and opposite force being just sufficient, by definition, to resist the counter-revolutionary force being applied by that space upon her in the manner described, there being no reason, of course, on her part, for her not to increase the force that she could apply in this way such that she would, in fact, continue in this manner to revolve clockwise around her longitudinal axis when viewed from the head rather than the foot, which is to say, when viewed from a position on the superior side of a transverse section through her body, as she had been hitherto, not, of course, that she would need to initiate this resistive force until that space, whose front was still in the process of elevating itself in relation to its rear, had attained a certain angle, which is to say, a certain degree of steepness, given, that is, that the breadth of her body (and that of most human and even humanoid bodies per se) was proportionately much greater than its depth, meaning, in short, that in circumstances in which it was arranged in a supine position, a steep angle would be required to tip such a body from its back or, were it arranged in a prone position, from its front onto one or other of its sides, such that she decided instead, instinctively and immediately, and despite now removing her right hand or, more specifically, her right palm from the base of that space, actively, in fact, to accentuate rather than to resist the counter-revolutionary force that continued to be induced in her by the front of that space elevating itself, or being elevated, in relation to its rear, by leaving her right elbow in situ on the base of that space to the right of her own supine torso, with the deployment of that vertex designed to enable, in short, greater leverage on her part, given the ongoing non-responsiveness of her lower limbs, in relation to the counter-clockwise revolution around her longitudinal axis when viewed from the head rather than the foot, which is to say, when viewed from a position on the superior side of a transverse section through her body, and which she now initiated by applying a force through it that was sufficient, despite the mismatch in the aforementioned relative dimensions of her body – despite, that is, its breadth being so much greater, relatively speaking, than its depth – decisively to switch the polarity of revolution in her body, to initiate, that is, this counter-clockwise revolution around her longitudinal axis when viewed from the head rather than the foot, which is to say, when viewed from a position on the superior side of a transverse section through her body, a motion she further accentuated by moving her right hand counter-clockwise both around the equivalent elbow – when viewed, that is, from her right – and around her longitudinal axis when viewed, as before, from the head rather than the foot, which is to say, when viewed from a position on the superior side of a transverse section through her body, such that it traced a curved trajectory around her torso, thereby shifting her centre of gravity slightly to her left, which, with the addition of the still-increasing backwards, upwards, or, from her perspective, leftwards, tilt of the space itself meant that she found herself on the brink of another tipping point, albeit one whereby her centre of gravity shifted from the infinite three-dimensional volume to the right of her base when viewed from the head rather than the foot, which is to say, when viewed from a position on the superior side of a transverse section through her body, to the infinite three-dimensional volume to its left, which, incidentally, removed, once again, the pressure that had been placed on her left hand and arm given that, in this transition, the right-hand side of her torso had, of course, elevated itself, or been elevated, such that that left hand and arm, which remained behind her, were no longer bearing that part of her body, with the pressure on her left shoulder increasing accordingly, at which point she was literally and metaphorically in a position to remove her right elbow from the base of that space, which is to say literally and metaphorically to transition back from using her right elbow to apply thrust to the base of that space towards using her right hand to apply thrust to its internal rear façade, with the relative dynamics within that space, in this interim between force applications upon surfaces that were, of course, at right angles to one another, being sufficient, she judged, all else being equal, to maintain her counter-clockwise angular momentum, which is to say that, despite being literally and metaphorically in no position, during this interim or hiatus, to use her right elbow or hand to apply pressure upon any of the internal façades of the eight- or twelve-sided three-dimensional space, given that the right elbow and hand were, as it were, then free-floating within that space – as that hand transitioned, that is, through the arm's straightening around that elbow and the wrist's bending in the process, in preparation for the contact of that hand, in the form, perhaps, of its palm or fingertips, with the internal rear façade of the eight- or twelve-sided three-dimensional space once again, just as it had transitioned previously, albeit in the opposite direction – although she found, as she judged her right hand to be approaching that surface, which is to say the internal rear façade of that eight- or twelve-sided three-dimensional space within which she remained, for now, enclosed, that the trailing edge of that enclosure actually commenced elevating itself – or being elevated – not though in relation to the leading edge, but rather in a way that was consistent with the continued increase in elevation of that leading edge such that both edges, now, were engaged in increasing their absolute elevations while maintaining, between them, a constant elevatory differential so that, as far as she could tell from her compromised and constrained vantage point within that mobile enclosure, the space's trailing edge had – perhaps inevitably – now entered, in a forward direction, upon the same upwards ramp or slope that its counterpart, the leading edge, had been occupying and ascending ever since her right palm had first touched down upon the base of that space to the right of her torso as a form of shock-absorber for the remainder of her body as the latter revolved clockwise around her longitudinal axis when viewed from the head rather than the foot, which is to say, when viewed from a position on the superior side of a transverse section through her body, although she still judged, despite concerns to the contrary, this abrupt elevatory action on the part of the trailing edge of the space to be, in fact, insufficient to prevent her from reaching her revised goal, given, that is, both the proximity, now, of the fingertips of her right hand to the internal rear façade, and the angular momentum still available to her from both the force she had applied via her right elbow to the base of that space and that of gravity supported by the ongoing angular disposition of the space itself, which remained, of course, broadly supportive of the counter-clockwise revolution around her longitudinal axis when viewed from the head rather than the foot, which is to say, when viewed from a position on the superior side of a transverse section through her body, in which her body continued to engage, despite that angular disposition no longer, now, increasing, such that she felt certain she would eventually turn fully to face the space's inner rear façade again, her right hand placed upon it, with the latter having traversed that inner volume via a series of swept paths resembling, if not replicating precisely, the mirror image, rotated through ninety degrees, of the route it had taken from that façade, the hand, wrist and elbow, in these trajectories, acting, she thought, like the weights at the end of a series of connected pendula, effecting the aforementioned motion, and she would continue rolling towards the rear of that space until, that is, she found herself, as she did now, back in her starting position, resting on her left side facing, at close quarters, the inner rear façade of what she regarded, now, as the relative safety of that dreadful enclosure, a stasis she monitored and maintained by ensuring that her right hand not only stayed in contact with that façade but, in addition, remained poised to increase, reduce or remove accordingly the force she had at her disposal, in response, that is, to the changing dynamics imposed upon her if not by me then by some unnameable – and seemingly unassumable – presence that is, perhaps, despite its rigours, worthy of preservation in its undifferentiated, non-subjectively inhabitable, non-objectifying, non-automated, unfocalised and fully unaffiliated combinatory form.

AMN
BEAC
ANDRE

SIAC
FIRE
MASON

Amnesiac Beach Fire

Andrea Mason

It is all useless, if the last landing place can only be the infernal city, and it is there that, in ever-narrowing circles, the current is drawing us.'

– Italo Calvino

In *Spiral Jetty* (1970), Robert Smithson lays out a 1,500-feet-long, 15-feet-wide, anticlockwise spiral walkway using 6,000 tons of black basalt rock and earth at the edge of the Great Salt Lake in Utah. Visitors are asked to leave no trace at the site – by taking their waste away with them, by not removing rocks from the work, by not making fire pits nor trampling vegetation.

Storyteller: She has tasked herself with visiting her local Integrated Waste Management Facility once a week for a year. She wants to know about waste, its relation to capitalism and climate change. She needs to understand the nature of it, the volume of it, like a storm chaser terrified of storms. She will examine the discarded goods with a dispassionate eye, in the way that a hospital consultant matter-of-factly dispenses with the person in front of them, writing a follow-up letter, for instance, which states that 'this pleasant woman' has a bone density suggestive of a fragility this same woman does not recognize. Will she accept the inferno, the inferno we form by being together, and become such a part of it that she can no longer see it? Or will she – and this option demands constant vigilance and apprehension – seek out and learn to identify who and what, in the midst of the inferno, are *not* inferno, then give them space, to let them endure?

Dialogue: *Spooky*, Denise says, when she tells her later. *Last week we had a dead cat and a dead dog.*

Rules: Denise is her portal into the dump. She writes her name into Denise's Visitor Book, and Denise gifts her a hi-vis vest and a red hard hat. Entry is via an open hangar. She is always careful to look left for exiting traffic (she has watched the health and safety video and signed off her compliance), and takes the pathway alongside a low aluminium barrier, which leads to a flight of metal steps up to a first-floor concrete concourse.

Tribe: Two JCB diggers, travelling in opposite directions, draw alongside each other. The driver nearest to her shouts across to the other driver, who is wearing ear protectors. George, a site worker wearing a scarf and woollen hat – *to keep the flies off* – shouts across to this driver.

Finite: TODAY, AT THE DUMP, the world is in the bin: a classroom globe, tossed into TVS & MONITORS, stands on its head, a round peg in a square crate in want of the hard angles of a TV or monitor.

> In *Viet-Flakes* (1966), Carolee Schneemann's film montage composed of Vietnam atrocity images plays on 14 old-school boxy TVs, which hang from the gallery ceiling; cables drape down like tendrils and spool on the floor around 14 DVD players. The world in TVs.

Sounds: DOWN THERE, IN DIGGERLAND, two site workers approach a stationary JCB. The man gets into the driver's seat; the woman stands by the passenger-side huge tyre – the door above it is open – and taps the side of the cab with a spanner: *tack, tack, tack*. The driver starts the engine and lifts the digger arm, tilting the bucket forwards and upwards, before drawing it back in, like someone doing Cat-Cow: head lifts, chest presses forwards, back arches (Cow); head curls in, back rounds (Cat). The woman moves away and leans against a blue, industrial-sized recycling bin where she continues to tap: *tock, tock, tock*.

Behaviour: George waves at her cheerily as she notates the TVs and monitors: BUSH, DELL, DAEWOO, SHARP, GOODMANS, JVC, SAMSUNG. She smiles and waves back.

Gestures: A JCB driver, the one George shouted to, is using the digger arm to bash down METALS, which sit in a container on the ground floor, making room for new bikes and scooters. A trolley catches in the teeth of the bucket. The digger arm bashes repeatedly against the side of the container in an effort to dislodge the trolley, like a horse kicking its belly to dislodge a fly. George flings his arms up and down. The driver presses the trolley against the inside edge of the container, and jerks the digger arm up. The trolley falls. George raises his arms in celebration.

Harvesting: George wheels a red trolley full of bikes and scooters to METALS.

Actions: A man gently floats pieces of bubble wrap and polystyrene packaging over the cubicle wall at HOUSEHOLD WASTE, a piece of which obscures a book's title. At WOOD & TIMBER, a woman throws in lengths of wood with abandon: a satisfactory *thwuck*, *thwack*, *crack*, as each item meets the criss-cross pile of Victorian pine doors, wooden pallets and broken-up particle-board kitchen cabinets.

Objects: TODAY, AT THE DUMP, in FRIDGES & FREEZERS, a HOOVER LINK washing machine stands alongside a FLYMO EASIMO lawn mower stands alongside an electric clothes dryer stands alongside an oven stands alongside a ZANUSSI ELECTROLUX. The appliances stand on the ground floor as she enters, where she can walk around them.

> In *In the Kitchen* (*Fridge*) (1977), Helen Chadwick stands coffined inside a tall fridge-freezer with an interior upholstered with white PVC. Chadwick's body is just visible through a layer of the PVC: the dark upside-down triangle of her pubic mound, the shape of her torso and thighs. Her head, uncovered, pokes above the top shelf. The lightbulb is on.

Stories: TODAY, AT THE DUMP, a hand-carved decorative rocking horse. As she walks further along the wall to get a better view she sees that the head has been sawn off.

Constructions: PLASTERBOARD and METALS sit side by side in large containers on the ground floor. Other categories (HARDCORE & RUBBLE, GARDEN WASTE, WOOD & TIMBER, HOUSEHOLD WASTE and CARDBOARD) are partitioned by concrete walls, which run down to the ground floor, down there, to the land of JCB diggers and crushers, and men and women with long-handled brooms.

Correspondences:

> In *Der Lauf der Dinge* (*The Way Things Go*, 1987), Fischli and Weiss harness the energy of never-ending collapse: wood and tables and bags of rubbish spin and turn and flip and fall; substances ignite and explode, drip and drop; chemical reactions cause explosions and eruptions, expansions and contractions; dust flies; fluids flow; chairs tip; tyres roll; carpets unfurl; planks topple; wheeled contraptions power along tracks; barrels barrel; sparks fly; oil burns; a weighted object on a string catches fire and flies around a central pole, like a comet circling a Swingball; clogs trundle; air gusts; a cardboard box floats. And *fin*: a volcano of white steam explodes out of a bucket.

Contraries: She watches Slovenian philosopher Slavoj Žižek in a YouTube clip of the 2008 documentary *Examined Life*. A dramatic soundtrack accompanies the camera as it moves down from a shot of industrial fluorescent strips to a heap of mixed waste: plastic bags and clothing. *This where we should start feeling at home. We are used to our waste disappearing, like shit*, Žižek says. *In fact, waste is our nature and we should love it. Love is not idealisation. True ecologist loves all this.* He gestures to a heap of plastic bottles as the camera pans to reveal that he too is standing in a London waste facility.

Discourse: TODAY, AT THE DUMP, in HOUSEHOLD WASTE, a copy of *The Tipping Point* by Malcolm Gladwell (2000). The paperback has

Andrea Mason

a yellow band, top and bottom of the front cover – pale and pissy, not unlike the colour of the stained patches of the mattress it sits atop. She presses her ribs against the cold dusty wall, as she leans in to read the subtitle: *How Little Things Can Make a Big Difference*.

Folk tale: A man, wearing a plaid suit jacket, offers two varnished wooden swords to a young man wearing a grey sweatshirt and black woollen hat. *I'd be happy for these to go to someone*, the man says. The young man carefully places the swords into the cab of his silver Transit van, parked alongside.

Narrative functions: TODAY, AT THE DUMP, in HARDCORE & RUBBLE, a handheld showerhead covered in dust pokes out from a broken-up concrete floor heaped against the retaining wall. Breeze-blocks sit heavily on top of the rubble. It is just six weeks since the earthquake in Turkey and Syria. For some twelve days she has woken daily to images of rubble and dust-strewn people and things – this being the timespan in which one might still expect to recover people alive from under the rubble. After this period, the story disappeared from news headlines.

> In *Regular/Fragile* (2002) by Liu Jianhua, a repetitious facsimile of everyday objects – shoes, toys, hot-water bottles, hammers, bags, mobile phones – cast in shiny white porcelain, cascade down the gallery walls, made in response, the gallery info says, to a series of aviation disasters that happened in China when the artist was going through a hard time.

Imagination: She imagines every person, everywhere, emptying out everything from their homes, turning the streets and roads the world over into one gigantic categorized and colour-coded artwork. In the BBC's *Sort Your Life Out* – a 2021 reality TV programme in which families clear their houses of all their possessions, and the show hosts lay everything out on the floor of a mega warehouse, in order to radically declutter – the families displace the problem of what to do with usable but unwanted items by taking them to charity shops,

Amnesiac Beach Fire

creating an endless feedback loop of donate, rebuy, lay out, donate, rebuy, lay out, donate, rebuy, lay out; a merry-go-round of buying and giving and buying and giving and buying and giving of goods, which we must love.

Patterns: Two pigeons flap around in circles in the arch of the roof of the cavernous hangar.

Entropy of language: LATER, AT HOME, in a dream, a woman is on a hospital trolley. She has three toad-like eyes. Her skin is warty. The woman stares at her. Beseeches. She is beseeching. She is *something*. The nurse talks as she inserts her hand into the woman's left eye socket and rummages inside the woman's face, in the same way we see vets' forearms shoving into cows' uteruses. Poor cow. Like in the 2021 documentary *Cow* by Andrea Arnold. Poor bloody cow.

Language as machine: On the PAINT trolley: Wickes Trade Silk Emulsion; Cuprinol Forest Oak One Coat Sprayable Fence Treatment; Crown Trade durable primer; Fads Super Value Vinyl Silk; Garden Deco Timbercare Red Cedar; Rustins Quick Dry Outdoor Clear Varnish; Radiator Durable Satin North Pole, low VOC content; Dulux White Mist Easycare Washable and Tough Matt; Wickes Wood Preserver; Dulux Natural Hints Jasmine White; Johnstone's Acrylic Durable Eggshell; Crown Stone White 6 Year Anti Mould Paint for walls and ceilings; Dulux Walls & Ceilings Chic Shadow; Dulux Endurance Polished Pebble; Cuprinol Less Mess Fence Care; Farrow & Ball Estate Emulsion Sulking Room Pink – a message on the lid reads: 'important instructions: make sure the colour of the paint is correct before painting'; Hammerite Radiator Paint: hard-wearing, resists yellowing.

Signs: Up here, a concrete wall the height of her ribcage is all there is between her and the waste; she looks over this wall as one might look over a cliff edge, to see what's been dashed against the rocks. In CARDBOARD, a flattened box says 'I AM UPSIDE DOWN'. In PLASTERBOARD, sheets of broken-up plasterboard have different coloured edgings: red and green.

In *Coral Reef* (2000), by Mike Nelson, a labyrinth of makeshift interconnecting spaces with rough plasterboard walls and scratched painted wooden doors have few enough objects in them to state transience, and just enough to project an identity of the inhabitants: a wall-mounted clock, a calendar hung on a nail, a camp bed with sleeping bag, a tall unattended wooden counter, a non-denominational shrine, a ship in a bottle, a prayer mat.

Combinatorial play: A large red wire crate contains CAR BATTERIES, inside which a brown dog finger puppet is categorically misplaced.

In *Orange Lion* (1991), by Paul McCarthy, a dirty toy lion sits sad-eyed, legs out in front, tail poking out – 'penis-like', writes Max Glauner in *Frieze* magazine – between its legs, left paw 'about to grab hold.' 'This little chap,' Glauner continues, 'clearly doesn't belong in the nursery.'

Labyrinth: LATER, AT HOME, she opens up her laptop. The screen moves as the episode of *Sort Your Life Out* she was watching before she fell asleep reboots. It's the part where the family come to see their stuff laid out on the floor of a mega warehouse, organized by category and colour, like a Tony Cragg sculpture. The family watch in wonder as the shutter goes up to reveal 111 bottles of nail polish, 80 packets of out-of-date medicine, 203 hair accessories and one thousand books.

In *Cold Dark Matter: An Exploded View* (1991), Cornelia Parker exploded and reconstituted a garden shed: shards of wood, wheelbarrow wheels, tattered wellington boots and bent bicycle frames are suspended by wires from the gallery ceiling, lit by a single bulb which creates shadow play.

Facsimile: TODAY, AT THE DUMP, a forest: pine prunings cover the concrete floor. The green against the grey reminds her of a sweatshirt she bought at H&M, attracted by a green forest transfer that contrasted pleasingly with the grey of the fabric. Back home, she found the sweatshirt too thick. She felt heavy. She improvised by rolling up the sleeves each time she wore it. Then, she chopped off the waistband and cuffs and slashed the neck, *Fame*-style. It was ruined: unreturnable, unfit for the charity shop, nonrecyclable. She stuffed it into a bin bag along with other similarly neutered items and sent it off to landfill.

> In *Make a Salad* (2008), Alison Knowles stands at a table, knife in hand, on the bridge of the Turbine Hall at the Tate Modern, and chops cucumbers, radishes and tomatoes to the accompaniment of a live orchestra. On a count, she throws the salad onto a giant green tarpaulin that covers the concrete floor, chucks over the dressing, and descends into the hall where she forks it into colanders from which the salad is served. Every time you eat a salad, Knowles says, you are performing the piece.

Imagined fortress: In SMALL APPLIANCES: a black boombox, a cassette deck, a kettle, a transistor radio, a portable PowerFoot, two coffee-makers, a fan heater, a toaster, a car tyre, seven bicycle tyres. The tyres are interlopers.

> In *Babel* (2001), Cildo Meireles stacked radios in a spherical tower, progressing through the different devices of the ages. The oldest styles – big, wooden, boxy – form three base layers. Smaller box shapes in metal and black plastic and smaller still silver-coloured plastic boxes with rounded edges form a series of concentric rings, some of

which sit proud of the vertical: the whole has the look of a thing with moving parts, like a camera lens. Tuned to different frequencies, the radios emit a cacophony of sound, calling her to listen.

Optimistic finale: In *Spiral Jetty: The Film* (2023), Robert Smithson runs along the earthwork. On arriving at the central inner point of the coil he gazes back at the spiral path and the landscape it sits within: the lake, the mountains. A sculpture has washed up on the beach: Mike Nelson's *Amnesiac Beach Fire* (1997), a circle of logs with red plastic triangles of fire stapled to them. A sign. A signifier. An object awaiting a storyteller.

PATIE
AVE
IPHGEN

IT S IS
FU AL
A BAAL

Images   News   Colposcopy   Coarse   Cervix   Fine   Olmtuz   Video   Maps   Shopping

Urgent message to all smartphone users – this is the road map to your Lamborghini!!!

Delivering a KILL SHOT to the $1.32 trillion big cable and internet giants… (click here to see a former Goldman Sachs banker's analysis)

Thousands of brand new 'mint' condition Ford trucks just sitting in a parking lot in Kentucky. Wanna know why?

>Oh, how far we whimsical lot have come
>and how much we've lost in the name of Progress.
>Old folk dances and life masks,
>where now there are death masks of old colonialists.
>Chunks fall off and into the plastic sea.
>Islands are surrendered to rubbish or (worse)
>tourism,
>so there are no more treehouses left for the three wizards who speak to using 'clicks'
>and baby talk.
>AGRRRR AGRRRR
>LAGGAGA
>AWAWOOO
>MAMA.
>
>Boomer Dad walks into Starbucks. This happens:
>
>CLICK here to apologize!
>CLICK here to be saved!
>CLICK here to forgive!
>CLICK here to forget!

Lil Pino's favourite food is *banana*

These Days Young People:
  — don't want to work in the restaurant industry anymore
  — want to be revolutionary neo-Utopic visionary thought leaders
  — want Nightly fire ceremonies with drums and feathered masks
  — want assurance their Spirit will be venerated by the community

But:
  — You still make better tips as a bartender or waiter and it's a good way to   1.   meet ladies.
  — You still make better karma as a shaman or medium and it's a good way to   meet angels.

That, or:
  — The price of cocaine is getting out of hand.

Don't want to get caught slipping so now's the time to pick the fluff off of your metaphorical slippers in time for the

                        Mass
                            Collective
                                    Psychic
                                             Crash!

Now who's controlling the narrative?

The Global Christ Consciousness Grid is buzzin'!
Go_get_bitcoin
Come on, quickly.
Get 22,255$ deposited into your account immediately.

Your money is in jeopardy.

They said:
                that
                they
                can't
                get
                me
                any
                thinner
                because it will cause the tumour to grow.

:(

Meet up with your old _____ [insert as appropriate] and they tell you:
        'I'm not the person you once knew.'
You listen, trying to be respectful of the new self they've found but inside you are thinking:

                You used to be famous for your careful, elegant output.
                        Poetic. Worthy of review.
                But you can't come up with anything other than
                      'angry' and 'visceral' these days.

Later that night, you watch a video that went viral months ago but somehow you missed it. A social media romantic had an out-of-body experience. You Wiki everything you can about her and think that even if you've never met, you're already intellectually co-dependent. <u>Conceptualizing in virtual space.</u>

Back in RL:
Had lunch (mega messy) then did a massive poo that went ev-ry-where. After the poo you

decide to put your whole fist down your throat and throw up over yourself and over me, so now we both smell of sick.

Two days and Shock Poppet's already gone feral. The dirty little grifter.

Yahoo! answers

WHAT DID MY DAD JUST SAY TO ME? I was listening to my iPod so I couldn't hear him. Out in the garden, sitting in puddles where moulds produce allergens, irritants and toxic substances. Inhaling and touching spores prompts asthma attacks. *Tha cuid de bacteria a 'seasamh gu nàdarra an aghaidh cuid de antibiotaicean.*

The occupants of grief – wailing children with no home nor shelter – can be found on the ninth floor with a shower that goes hot/cold/hot and a toilet that honks each time it's flushed.

(Once you lie to me imma always think u lying)

Those niggas that didn't even ride? No love lost. Your own family can be toxic as fuck and wonder why you don't wanna be around them

:>> self-recognition through the other <<:

Incoming tsunami > Linking the local with the global > Recording by the late Porton 'Electronic' Bent. (It is extremely appropriate, then, that someone like him, who links the modern and the traditional, would come to such a sorry end, out on the Isle of Skye – the last place in the British Isles where it's still possible to be philosophical.)

Learn Crofting/Off Grid/Self-sufficient
ASDA – 10 miles as the crow flies but at least a day's travel there and back.

We are all still trying to find ways of writing that ward off the more negative influences of the publishers. (Congratulations on getting this far.) We've got something you've been trying to find for a while, to restore motivation in a world that is designed to wear you out. (If, that is, you are seriously striving to obtain an alternative.)

btw, not a *single person* has compensated me to check in on you — @Wahdaddin_|Trotpostinsky

I want to be heroic but I also plan to survive.

Coming-of-age function creep: echoes of society at the start of the 19th C., when bawdiness was replaced with prudence as people lost their lands, their means of production, and became dependent on the church and then the state.

>	Anti-stress home decor app – Fantastic, innovative, contemporary
>	Ideal Excellence.
>	Future Highlander in neo-woodland
>	Join the custom lobby.
>	No street sweepers
>	Add Sarge #9259858 to get added.

Only difference is that at the start of the Industrial Revolution peasants weren't inundated with press releases overstating the significance of the Industrial Revolution. *See*, The Little Mermaid holds her teddy, staring out the French windows of the nursery at a passing jellyfish. Yes, I'm the gatekeeper and also a hater. I'm also holytrinitybikini's favourite princess and the most interesting person in the world.

one of the marks or depressions

People also ask:

☐ What does punctate mean medical?
☐ Does punctate mean small?
☐ What is the meaning of being on time?

Reach us by all means available NOW. (That's what we learned in Live Chat Class.)
I will write papers for you to help you get an A grade.

Karl Marx will not have sex with you. Stalin will do you doggy-style on the rug to the sound of the low hum of the Overground gliding into a station where the platform is too short. 'The doors in the first four carriages will not open. Please move towards the rear of the train to exit.' The pre-recorded announcement is made in a woman's voice. 'Would Mr Sands please report to the operation room. Mr Sands.'

You are not responsible for the emotional state of others around you just because you watched a reel from augustknoxcoaching.

This can show up as:

People Pleasing
Perfectionism
Hypervigilance
Always making sure others are happy
Pretending you don't have needs

Another fine example of Prussian terror tactics.

Signs of a weak man: Has a TikTok account, Smokes weed, Porn addict, Broke, Desperate for Women: Do you agree with this? (Yes/No)

No cameras on on the scene means no CCTV. We are free. At last! Like that first day of lockdown, when we watched that man climb that tree. The police came and they were like, 'Come down, we're not going to arrest you', but the guy in the tree wouldn't come down and told them, 'The last time the police told me they weren't gonna arrest me, they arrested me.' The police tried to climb the tree to get him but they couldn't get up nearly as high as the man. Eventually they gave up and left him there.

All the Gnostic going on so much.
It does, it manifests. A torture room, shootings in a street.

Mum says I lost the plot,
(At least I never lost my crop).

I'll turn up and say my existing is 'forged abahd id'.

The commissariat planted a van in the middle of Green Lanes to clear the thing for Gentoo Greenlee. It's when the Kurds were fighting ISIS. It was, it was kind of deserted. Their being into Hara[1], non-Labour. Every night they bring it all in. It's fentanyl, mostly, but it's still them doing it. It's not worse but it's definitely more complicated. There's still those kind of white hoodies types, you know, eh-oh Tommy Robinson and all that, but it's getting less. It's more outside of London. They say 'Muslim paedo rape gang' but the guy was actually a Sikh.'

Manchester brags with the miserable ones: *Complete pedestrianisation.*

Lesson from teen cousin who lives in L.A.: when teens have big parties they make a new insta account - for the party - and people have to request to follow it, and an approval means you can come to the party??? and you have to show your insta to get into the party (there is security).

My friend blocked her ex on Twitter, Facebook, call/text and literally every conceivable form of social media but hey, the heart wants what the heart wants. reddit.com/creepyPM

People will find their own uses for tools.

It was signed, told me wrong, by The Maskless and Dr Witts-'is-name. God knows all the best people are objecting to the End of the World. I did not like all that, not X Factor, what do they call it? The anti-the-anti-end-of-the-worlders.

This generation makes you wanna fuck with nobody fr

A total of no BLACK BLACK BLACK (careers). You cannot turn up as a white guy. Why is ish unhappy?

Because I was born to play sorry keys with the highs.

Main main main obsession is the cupboard wit the pipes in it. I don't know if there's a leaking pipe or if it is an old leak that hasn't dried out.

Vinegar and baking soda on Dido.
Breezeblocks and rubble.
No rebar.
Good night.

All reserves of strength harvested.
Bot Time: irrational hope.

---

1   Hara is one of the many names of Shiva, a principal deity of Hinduism and the supreme deity in Shaivism. As Hara, Shiva is 'the one who destroys evil.' On its own, Hara is a Sanskrit word that means 'removing', 'taking away' and 'destroyer.'

Mysticism (less irrational due to the elephant he'd encountered back before everything that made sense).

Highly recommend playing at .5 speed because he's young but has such big bags under his eyes. A coin held between finger and thumb.
Words rolling over tongue emphasize **total abandonment**.
Once upon a time, stuff to do: pay rent, brush teeth, empty washing machine. Owing.

And what of his friends?
The postman, who had wheedled his way into the man's affections, and that friend of his mother's who always smelt like ketamine. That smell, like emptiness, metal. And the Raving Beauty who had begged him, 'Drive me to Morley's, I'm hungry.' And he had. Had bought her chicken. What happened to you between now and then?

Mind leaping across vast chasms, body restrained? Yes, arms tied down and underneath an enormous oblong of AstroTurf. Feel its pricks.

And, the sky relents.
And, there is no time.
And, a wane orange crossed in inverse tiger clouds.
And, there is no camera.
And, a voice that sounded like it belonged to one of the miniature Pakistani rudeboys who used to hang around Brick Lane.
And, there is no caption.
And, it is a prank.
And, there is no copyright.
So, use it however you think best.
And, longing for a roast dinner, if only The Infinite Observer could stop thinking about himself for five fucking minutes.
And, get a grip, take a trip. Here are some guidelines:

    1: Don't forget the kid in the corner writing the words.
    2: Keep your buttons done up to the top.
    3: Don't listen to electric.
    4: Remember there are always five golden rules.
    5: And the last one you have to figure out for yourself.

Downloaded a scanned book and was unaccountably moved to tears by this connection to an anonymous scanner of African folktales, reimagined and broadcast on Netflix, *Death by a Million Uncles*. You deserve a good sitcom. Bakhmut village after the battles. That's what it had been. The girl, smelling of regret. She had done something to him. Had left him in the (disputable) care of these child gangsters. He could still hear them chuckling as he freed himself from his bounds and sniffed out his surroundings. Blind like a little mole, testing the corners, feeling what material the walls were made of – flimsy stuff.

Chilli is ableist.
Stew is racist.
Queso is fatphobic.
French onion soup denies the Armenian genocide.
'Are you sure he's ready?' said one voice, drooping from a peak of squeakiness to something deeper, subterranean sinister.
'No one's ever ready', replied a second voice, 'that's the point.'

Iphgenia Baal

Dress for the job you want, somewhere in North Ossetia.

That's why the internet is so dangerous and so much 'all in' behaviour with banks and stock markets trying to buy it all and take over the system.

> Text: The elephant in the room is insider trading during WW1 + WW2 by investment banks.
> Text: Proper Bond-villain behaviour
> Text: If the details of that come out… as in, the actual evidence… it would be chaos.
> Text: The scale of corruption is immense.
> Text: Functional government would see these cases being brought up like Nuremberg war trials and a major redistribution of wealth and companies getting shut down. Instead we have Glencore doing very well for its shareholder.
> Text: Even Auschwitz Buna-Werke was kept running by the USSR after WW2. They needed synthetic rubber.
> Text: Governments worldwide have been notified of what is coming next.
> Text: Love from, Esoteric bot

NounEdit · A preliminary treaty or contract

Fake has become so acceptable that people get offended when you keep it real 💯

We can't hear you. You're muted.

Do you want to experience the sensation of eternity?

Work your ass off.
Change the language.
Don't ever be famous.

CASHLESS SOCIETY IS NEXT!

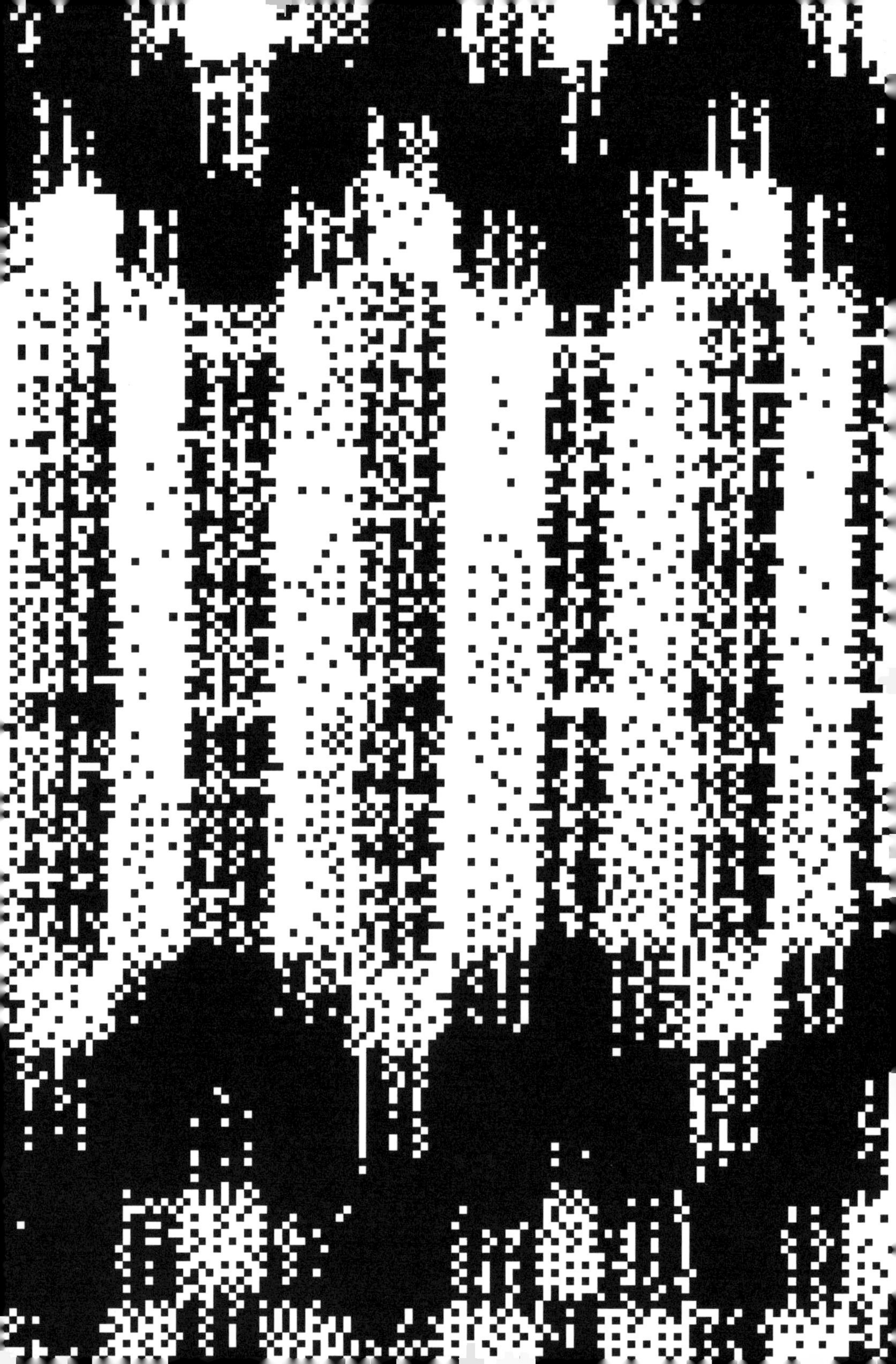

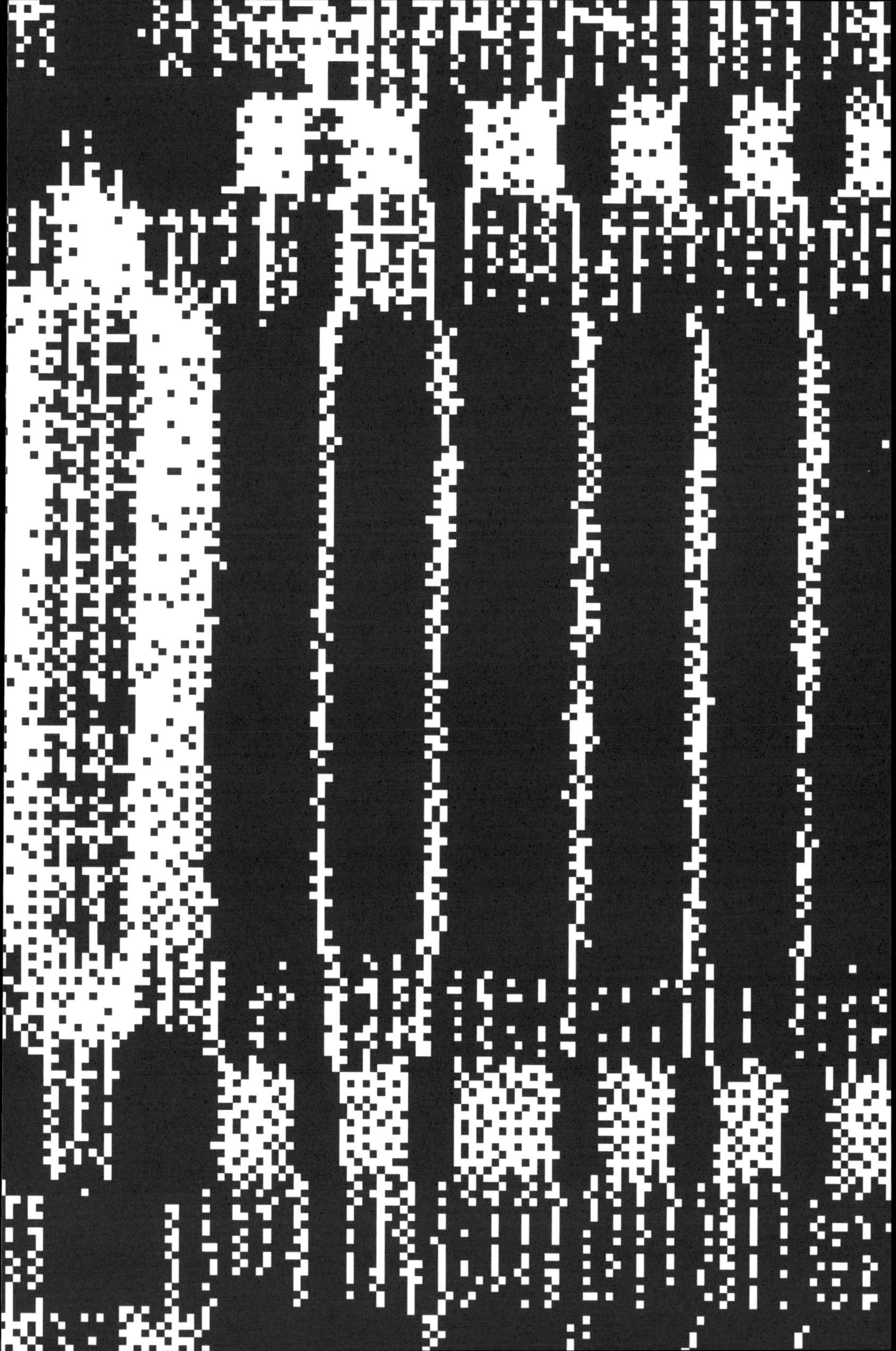

SOPRANO
THEY ARE
GREEN AND
ABOUT

TIC

MACHINE PALMERS
SOMEONE IS TO BE-
GIN

Soprano machine
They are in Palmers Green and someone is about to be —

Tice Cin

Session 3: One week before period

— Hot!
— OK, sorry.
— Hot, hot, sorry!
— I know it hurts, but don't move, just tell me.

She breathes to catch up, her breathing, like night-gasps, too visible. Heat travelling through teeth like numbness. It is as though she is swallowing the heat. Travelling. Coughing without being able to move the face.

She needs to move to the legs. Don't listen to her when she says to hold your top lip down, that makes the skin thinner and it hurts more. Why more pain on the right than the left? Why do I always feel like this woman's trying to con me? Unnecessary, just for laughs, just to kill time till her lunch break. Had to be me.

Extra ultrasound jelly squeezed on the thighs. Lying back, she is a client. A black tunic leans against her. A car alarm goes off outside and there is shouting from the lobby, from a receptionist to a car owner. Someone leans against the opaque glass window front from outside briefly, then moves away. The noise of their body against the glass seems as though it is inside the room.

— I'll keep putting more.
— That's good.

Legs go slack. Thighs into the tissued bed.

— Don't move.
— I relaxed too much, didn't I?
— Hmm.
— Am I more fidgety than normal?
— No — it's your first time isn't it? I'm Jayda.
— Second…
— You saw Sophiya last time?
— Tell a lie, it's my third. With you as well. Only.
— Hmm.
— Hot!

Leg kicks out. The gun is knocked and then pulled back into place in the Soprano machine. Whizz-snapping back into a hole.

— It's because you didn't shave close enough and your ones are very coarse.

— Sorry. Honestly I have a 9 o'clock by 2pm.
— Well it might never actually work for you because of your hormones.

A yellow disposable gets caught on a second yellow disposable, blades interlocuting. One is shaken loose into a bucket for sharps. Her bikini line starts to get shaven. Roughly and striking blood. Gel on top. The gun starts again, running over the crease between different softs, towards the edge of lace. Pinched between fingers, she is now conscious of the underwear she chose for today. She has sweated during the appointment and she wishes she had worn something less punishing. The last person who saw her in these described them as 'camel-toe sexy'. To mean: too small, but okay just this once. The jelly has seeped past the treatment area and has now wet the material, patches of underwear going from purple to black, tautening against her. Jayda has a tattoo on her ear.

— Hot!
— OK.

She pauses then carries on after two seconds, maximum. Soon, the jelly is red.

— Sorry, that's tickling.
— A lot of people say that.

Frowning, Jayda finishes one area, and before moving onto the next, wipes the jelly off with a stick. She then takes a large square of folded tissue and wipes it along the bikini line, close to the edge. The blood on the cloth, when pressed, resembles an inkblot test or a nightmare graph. Rorschach.

Shapes in tissue. Leak. Can't fix them. This must be a memory, a silk sheet. Skin pressing. Folding in like cellophane out the microwave. A lover runs across my forehead. What are you doing there? The tissue could melt on my face and I wouldn't mind. I wouldn't mind any of this. Too many things. She is sexy though. I wonder if she's had a BBL or if she bangs gym. Leaning over me now. I don't know how to hide this.

Session 4: After taking 4 instead of 2

Big smile. A perm, dyed red. Tunic with a stain on the breast pocket. Nipple piercing shouting through the fabric.

— Hi I'm Sophiya. Would you say you've been getting successful results? Has Jayda been advising you on how to look after yourself after sessions? You been putting sun cream?
— Yeah, I put sun cream. I put Vitamin E oil after my sessions too.
— Didn't she tell you? No oil! Clogs your pores. No anything actually. You need to leave it like three days. Before we start, you haven't taken anything have you?
— No, just ibuprofen.
— Oh well we can't do anything on you if you've taken ibuprofen. It could burn you. Didn't Jayda tell you? Anything with aspirin in it makes you sensitive to the light.
— Forget me, forget me, it wasn't ibuprofen. It was paracetamol.
— Are you sure? It could really burn you.
— It was paracetamol.
— Okay if you say so. Well let's start on your legs then.

White lines are softly drawn into her skin until she is segmented into trapeziums. Sophiya takes a lot of time on each area. She traces around the upper thigh, a border just past the pelvic bone. It should tickle.

The legs go easy. Barely a remark. Turn left. A phone alarm goes off.

— I have to go outside to move my car. I won't be long.

Jayda wouldn't do this. Is she in the other clinic? This girl has different perfume. Girls with different perfume come out to test you, get you to line up the smells and choose. Pick the one that looks like it's a glass bottle, these girls softer than cans.

She watches Sophiya leave, a McDonald's Little Miss Curious free keyring toy shakes with her as she goes. The jelly is starting to slide down her thigh. Look around. She scans:

A Doctor's Stock Checklist. Make sure all of the below are in all Doctors rooms for them to be able to carry out treatments. Refer friends cards. Upgrade Me Experience. Treatment plan card. Treatment menu. Special offers. 50% off facial card. After care advice. Complete doctors daily injectable stock sheet. Fridge temp card in fridge. Fridge temperate sheet on top of fridge (always check temperature). Appropriate product for treatment and extra (Fillers + Botox). Gauze swabs 10 x 10 1 pk. Sterets 1 box. Hyrdex Pink (Pink chlorohexidine gluconate 0.5%, 200ml. Bd microlance 3 x 1 pack. 5ml syringes.

— Sorry yeah. Let's go again.

Tissues x 2pk. Vinyl gloves Powder free (Small & medium). Baby wipes x 1pk. Spirigel complete 500ml x1 Bacteriostatic NS 0.9% 30ml x 3 (for Botox). Green syringes 1ml x 1 box. Baxter Connecters x 10. Pink/ Green or Orange needles x 1 box. Post procedure cream TEOXANE (or amica cream). Viscoderm Cover Up Dark x 1. Viscoderm Cover Up Light x1. LMX cream (numbing cream) x 1. Cool sense (ice stick) freezer x 2 (CHARGE). DermaSculpt 25Gx40mm x 1. DermaSculpt 25Gx50mm x 1. White Pencil. Sharpener. Surgical Masks. Pens (Black ink). Mirror. iPad/ Tablet. Couch roll. Yellow sharps bin (For syringes). Botox continuation sheets. Filler continuation sheets. Profhilo continuation sheets. Post-care sheets. Weekly to be completed by a manager. Any doctors if short on the day please inform a member of management to top up. Page 1 of —

— Are you sure you can't feel that?
— I can feel it, but it's fine.

She turns to the machine and raises the fluence to 8.

— And now? You can't feel that?
— I can feel it. That's it though.
— You know you can't take ibuprofen before a session. Are you sure you haven't taken anything? I'm about to move to a more sensitive area.
— No ibuprofen, I promise.
— Have you been watching Love Island this year?
— I have. The baby episode got me broody.
— You got a man?
— No.
— I've been with my boyfriend for five years, and you know — our people — that's wedding bells. But I want to travel first still. Don't mean to be funny but it looks like I'm squirting ketchup all over your legs!
— You plating me up?

The rivulets of clear jelly come out of the squeeze bottle, all lined up in a row. They catch the light of the overhead lamp and become pearlescent. The gun presses them down four by four until the thigh is glossed.

— When you smell the burning don't you just feel great?
— What burning?
— You can't smell that? It's amazing. Satisfying. Means it's working.
— Ah you know what, I can smell it now. Are you sure that's okay?

෴

Stop talking. Just trying to chase it. Thunder looping in my head. Warned him before the session I'd be arriving yawning from lazor. No, it isn't tiring. Therapeutic only. He says, that's good, you need to be ready to drink. Jayda's sessions have more perks. Good quiet. I go unseen. Chit-chat lost the flow. Tracing backwards but the window of opportunity is small. Paper ripping, shapes snagged, couldn't catch the thought.

Session 5: Sweated through from running for the bus

— Is it inside buttocks today?
— Yes, and the rest. How was your holiday?
— Oh yeah it was alright, thank you. How'd you know? Who did you see last time then, Sophiya?
— I did.
— Is she your usual girl?
— No, this will be my fourth one with you today.
— Have you ever considered doing your arms?
— No, I like my arm hair actually.
— You like it? I always thought it made women look like a lesbian or something.
— I like it.
— What about your back? It seems silly to do your bum and not your back.
— Just this lot for now. To be honest I can't afford another area.
— OK.
— I've been getting these breakouts. Is it because I've been doing something wrong?
— No, they're just ingrown hairs. You need to scrub more.
— I'll do that.
— If you come to our sister clinic I can offer you 50 percent off a buttocks facial.
— How much would that be?
— Well it's the 'Radiance' one. We do it really nice. £50.
— That's okay thank you, I'll just get some type of rock salt and do it myself.
— I think you should come in to get it done. You probably scrub the wrong way.
— I scrub in circles, isn't that the right way?
— That's fine but we scrub professionally, the proper right way. Okay let's do your front now.

She wears her surgical mask with her nose out. One of her lash extensions is winking to free itself. When she leans in, I feel like she's zooming out, it's like she's about to swoop over me. I feel like she is going to fall. Don't let this get to you. The jelly feels nice still. Round and round. No, it doesn't hurt. Skin shaking. Hot. Hot! I wish I could tell someone about this. Focus. Don't be that girl. Allow it. There's no hiding this. Round and round. Lucky the air-con is on. Start saying it's cold from now, so she thinks less. No pain, all I can feel is a gradual rise. Hard to hide.

❦

She has been sat on the toilet for thirty minutes, ever since coming away with so many hairs. You're not allowed to pull them, but if you hold them one by one between your nails, they come loose as though you never tried. She counts them coming free. Thirty-two, tired. She lines them up on a square of toilet paper and considers pressing them down with glass to preserve the sight. Later that night, the results are complimented. Her legs are so soft, so sleek, never felt legs like that before. All it took was a year and a bit.

⚘

The six-month top-up should really stop after a couple of years. The procedure doesn't work for some people though. Especially not people from certain parts. Enough of an impression to state its case, just enough to keep it going. Inside buttocks today. Stiletto nails this time make it harder to pull them apart.

Fucking impossible to keep them apart.

– Sorry.
– It's okay, must mean you've been doing your squats.
– Don't play, there's no muscle here!

There is a shop sign that, with patience, can be read backwards through the window from the bed. A woman in Shellac blonde hair with teeth. 'Why wouldn't you choose to be the best YOU possible?' All services available. A water bottle is knocked over by one girl leaning towards another on the table. There is no response to it.

Through goggles, the water looks like it has been left there to trick someone. Purple and swirling. There must be a specific genre of ambient music designed to distract you from pain. When a neck is turned on its side for too long, it can only hear the things it shouldn't hear. Behind the water bottle is a poster that promises safe, effective, long-lasting results. It shows an anterior view of the head and neck muscles. Temporals slash their way from ear to crane. The bit between the eyebrows and eyes is called 'procerus'. Not everything is red muscle. There is also the thyroid cartilage of the larynx, which is blue and closest to the clavicle, which is the colour of bone. Underneath all the rippling muscles are six different filler companies that sponsor the clinic. To the right of this, a lip chart. The *Mary*. Subtle. Natural enhancement. *Chanel*. Boost. Slight volume with slight definition. *Megan*. Plump. Fuller volume. *Rulic*. Fuller volume and definition. It goes on until it reaches the *Angelina*. Ultimate cupid. Maximum volume and definition. The *Angelina* is on sale. Above is an avatar with five faces marketing the facial aesthetics that come with a combination of dermal filler and Botox injections. Non-invasive solutions for: a gummy smile; jaw reduction; dimpled chin; vertical neck bands. The avatar, green-gold, has an ambiguity to it that almost blurs a viewer's eyes. It looks back at you.

— I was thinking I'd seen you before.
— Yeah you have Jayda.
— I actually can't believe it! Babe would you just pull them open more otherwise it's going to hurt. Don't stretch the skin though.
— Sorry.
— So you do the breakfast show don't you? I saw you on the way over here you know.

— What?

Straight pretty. We fall in pavement sides. Rest as if sleepy, my body shutting down. Suddenly she's less pretty, think I preferred her before. Preferred her quiet. Trust it to be now. Nails nice to make you trust me. Trust it to be now. Hair to silk, you think I'm clean. Smell of skin and she knows me. Back press she's in too close. Glad I took three. Fuck I'm hungry. Swear there's a sheep folk-dancing on my toes. Small elves plait its wool. Looking at my toes again.

— Yeah on the billboard, right where I park my car. You do it with that girl, the one with the funny hair?
— And that's when you recognised me?

She is passed fresh rows of tissue and wipes herself off, leaving clumps on the bed behind her; they form a circle around her goggles.

— No when you come in today I saw you had the same nails on, then I looked and looked. Anyway I followed you on Instagram — are you gonna follow me back? That's my dog in the picture with me. It's Jayda with a 'J' not a 'C'.

– I'll follow you back.
– It's funny you don't look like your photos in a big way, I wouldn't have clocked you.
– That's so funny innit.
– Alright well I'll see you next time hun, I've swapped it so you're not with Sophiya, you're with me. It's the best machine at the Hadley Wood clinic.

Post-session

Every body-con photo is liked. Three out of five stories are responded to with heart eyes. They are mutuals with two exes. For the first couple of days, Jayda doesn't accept her follow request back. When it's accepted, her profile tells how she got married and that she turned thirty with balloons. She has one child and her husband (up till recently, her ex) always looks bored in his photos. Her recent holiday with friends shows her with her girls illuminated by hotel glass. Her toes are glitter grey, just like two sessions ago. A turtle is on the balcony behind her. They wear matching bikinis, hers nearly as small, and in one photo a teenage girl walking past in the background is staring at her thong.

Familiarity starts to reveal itself as she scrolls further down. A slashed eyebrow, messy bun. School uniform and so. Jayda from two years above, who used to have a face that looked constantly disgusted and held a library monitor position for eight months before the eyebrow slash. In-session she hid disgust well. Or perhaps awareness of eyes gets lost in pain. Another top-up seems out of the equation now, and there are other clinics, less local.

| Soprano machine | They are in Palmers Green and someone is about to be – 205 |

BEDLAM
BUF
STEVE B

AND ITS
ERS

ARBARO

Bedlam and Its Buffers

Steve Barbaro

The Commander-in-Chief's in the gutter. The haste; the ceding. The calculated plummeting. The Commander-in-Chief's holed up in a bunker—the term *competence* pervades my own musings' crawlways all the same. Because the competence in question—is this not an eminently resilient competence? Something obliged by the cinched chain of yesterdays ever-vomiting new anarchy from the belly of today? Oh but this competence…… this competence the citizenry really needs……it's a *capacité* of which few are competent to even conceive. In light of order's essential retentions…… and amidst chaos's dizzying metamorphoses……but a choice few of us are fit to filter for what's necessary—The Commander-in-Chief down there fetching spooling threading, say. The Commander-in-Chief descending like a termite. The Commander-in-Chief self-administering pythonlike strangulating curlicues of cogitating. Yet far be it from me to indulge the fancy that……pure unfettered competence might also be the very reason The Commander-in-Chief is summoning me?

She always used to ask about you, my Mentee was some weeks back of a sudden insisting. *She always used to prod and pry and query*. Then one poolside day: *she's still in fact quizzing and canvassing—*
      The prawns crowned the plates like my bloodorange divingboard crowning one of this coolly choppy island's horizontal anomalies. *She's*

always grilling……pumping……needling. Yep: this local island space is ever-in-sight of crags crowning the hills themselves crowding the looming adjacencies not those of the sea. And lounging there whilst freeing my thighs of an onionlaced ham puffpastry's remnant flakes……I found myself conjuring lost thoughts of Sickstee. *Sickstee*, my Mentee kept huffing as if to eradicate the very forgetting of my forgettings. (My Mentee often does indulge such fidgetry upon serving a meal of her own devising.) *Sickstee*, *Sickstee*, my Mentee seethed through consummately cosmetic winds like a hymn to some impossibly non-variable polity. (Oh but those old mindclogging memories of Sickstee shredding documents in my spouse's villa after shooing forth shrieking midteens.) Yet in this case……my Mentee's labor seemed sufficiently taxing to permit her the indulgence of a presence whose absence was itself of a certain willed verisimilitude if not veracity.

    Sickstee is a very capable and at times prodigious entity, I allowed, before masticating more than one asparagus cake. *No one in their right mind would proffer any counterclaim.*

    Demonstrations were reaching a kind of second boiling point in those days. The algorithm used for calculating certain public health benefits not to mention permissions for public gatherings had of course long since been implementing historical info scraped from elder modular subsidiaries such as Sickstee and even newer more modestly memorious modular subsidiaries like my Mentee. But now……the majority of the parliament as well as the very palace-storming citizenry were doubly seething at the fact that this same data had already prevented thousands of people from casually leaving our country and/or even reentering.

    I myself—I could not dignify all the fussing and mussing! If any and every iteration of casual data gathering was not achieved would not some other less convenient (see: bureaucratic) process necessarily have to fill the infovoid? Nary a few allies and/or client-states were sufficiently clear-eyed to coordinate with our government on this policy; and our Commander-in-Chief stood pat in proclaiming that in light of all of the up-bubbling protests, there was no choice but to once again employ Section 3-dash-3 of the constitution—this time, to detain dubious would-be border crossers with exclusively executive ease… Plus I was anyways consumed with my own proceedings—unnumbing my all-too-recurringly numb feet, not least. Why else would I—unlike the mainland riffraff burning garbage and flailing—be loitering near the pool all day? If the brain is The Commander-in-Chief of the body it seemed my nether regions' toe-rabble was triumphing. The unthinkingness of cumulus……the windswept pool's endless self-transportings. My very daydreamings birthed obscenely indiscrete apparitions of mobility. Skyscrapers on chassis; jetties cruising freeways. Motion's very absence sure can be a consummately detached mechanism of unfixity. But the actual *engourdissement* would only cease whilst I was swimming or even merely sitting mid-deck and splish-splashingly dangling the whole toe-to-heel axis would-be-drowningly.

Sickstee and her ilk entail such an impudent velocity of insight, I sighed whilst scrutinizing swordfish-chunk-stacked plates. *By the precipitousness of their logic it's as if any old dolt might well coddle the earth's very core sans deferring to intervening geologies—*

And obviously I could have graced a beach's face—but who knows what hoi polloi you find washed up around the sea. I'd been in therapy ever since my spouse's passing but would that the therapy did not exacerbate the numbing. A confidante—my best and really only trustworthy intimate, Saverina, long since fled abroad for our citizenry's inconstancy—even suggested I visit a hypnotist but……I don't believe in all of that scary jerry. With one eminently feeling foot out of the veritable nation-door Saverina what's more cut me a deal on her own Mentee—indulging a brand new one would've been silly what with all of the expenses of my new retreat. And these Mentees—there's a reason their price range is equivalent to that of a yacht of fifty feet. Repairing car engines; fixing gutters and plumbing. Even rendering the so-called poolman obsolete. And not only are the memories of these new series modular subsidiaries inherently circumscribed—the overall thingies are streamlined to constantly cultivate a programmatically pleasant state of exhaustive practicality…

Honey, I in fact soon poolsidely informed my Mentee most expositorily, *honey—I am just going to get out of this here pool promptly—*

And I'll be damned if it wasn't with the noblest of mechanical instincts that my Mentee waltzed over and towel-caressingly administered to my feet. The caressing, processing. The faux-fingered-ness, fingering. The ensuing gesturing could indeed be best described as a kind of hyperconcentrated strangling. And those components known as *ankles*—I mean those two dumb hunks of bone, featureless, skinfaced, somehow almost shameless in their circumscribing functionality—yes these bleh-load-bearing entities were as if twin wombs from which twin engine-brains were birthchoked all but out of nothing.

The noun *decree*. The adjective *mandatory*. The very question of will—of stakes. Yes yes The Commander-in-Chief down there sifting. Compiling. Tabulating—*ordering*. Certainly not copulating; indubitably non-idling.

Inputting parliamentary-storming perfidy......and me myself...... catching a mainland ferry. Breathing musing heeding. Motion against fixity; stillness versus *mobilité*. The sea's unseemly incalculability... And The Commander-in-Chief all the while perfecting the terms of societal necessity. The word *balance*; the term *future*. The singular objective fact of one person's superiority... Plus the concomitant confidence to pluck the very citizenchords comprising the harp that is democracy. Yes the lone brave elected configurer configuring a society-beyond-configuring. An accountant or two in tow too—maybe? What with the files the folders. What with the data—the shootings. The citizens: the arrays. The boundaries—the *strings*.

She asks about you within 200000 milliseconds of our conversing. I'd strolled out to the hills and brought my decidedly speed-adept Mentee along as a kind of sensory auxiliary. *Sickstee's always saying boy oh boy we had some great times and wouldn't it be swell if we could once again meet...*

I was in fact running as I heard this—running being otherwise as beyond my competencies as navigating the riffraff-flooded mainland streets. The cragcaked hills cascaded as if according to the very *clonkclonk* of my feet; and by the end of my forays you better believe I'd unlocked that good old sweat-bestowed profusely world-embracing feeling.

Well, I informed my Mentee, *for all of your help with my foot you most definitely deserve a reward. How's about we have Sickstee flown out here for a few days. Shipping's on me!*

Mind you—my joy regarding my Mentee's feet-fix was indeed so great that I overlooked any downsides regarding Sickstee. Naturally: my Mentee is fed the historical thoughts of other modular subsidiaries. It's strange but......summons by elder model modular subsidiaries are seemingly the only trigger for such newer model emoting. Apparently this networking effect redoubles the practical knowledge of all included modular subsidiaries......even though it has been achieved despite rigorous computative efforts to the contrary? (The detachment of *discretion* from what's *discrete* seems a colonizingly recurring fact of modern living.) But as for me......I felt sated after having been reassured (and re-reassured) that my Mentee forgot whatever she may have known about the non-task-based aspects of my non-modular-subsidiary life before my Mentee started working for me and so......within a few more solicitously summery weeks I was doing my damnedest to humor Sickstee's old-times-conjuring mid-kitchen musings.

The dictation—the civility. The reminders of hobnobbing—of governing. The eminently centered unfettered sociality not to mention: the enforced revival of elder connections as if failure to calendrically refresh kindredness was the worst form of heresy... But more than mere nostalgia what was soon at hand was a veritable cataclysm of epistemology.

Ambassadors, MPs, longstanding auxiliary functionaries—I usually have my Mentee take on such correspondings. Agency heads, media moguls, PR chiefs—a gist enters my Mentee's range of hearing and my Mentee replicates the gist in messageform with virtuosic ease. But the accelerated avalanche of dispatches, sheesh... A missive demanding my presence even managed to materialize with a forthrightness verging on the obscene. The candidate for whom the appearance was ostensibly necessary had campaigned for me many times and was now insinuating that I might well be over my spouse's passing.

Sickstee, I beckoned with Sickstee-like forwardness from my living room one sunny day. *Sickstee—you are not having any involvement in my current communications now, are we?*

A coyly self-cloying mechanical gaze.

Sickstee?

A wryly me-prying regimental gaze.

Your numb feet were a kind of companion if not proxy, the thing had the nerve to say. *Your spouse's suicide birthed a need for company. Wonts like these are just as much a matter of utility as of intimacy. After all: you yourself were not without responsibility. The falsehoods; the downplaying. The blatant forays into the burial of history. The numbness was like a mechanism siphoning everything you were feeling. Siphoning—and thereby alleviating. As soon as the numbness in fact came to my attention I knew the numbness was equal parts lover and teacher, substitute and deputy. Not least because the numbness was a kind of reservoir for everything that fell beyond the purview of thought and speech—*

And when my Mentee rematerialized, my Mentee most certainly witnessed me grabbing Sickstee......until Sickstee grabbed me when I redoubly cinched the thing and this time not by the appendage but by the skinless throat as the skinless throat claimed *but I was the one who suggested your Mentee rub your feet that was me that was me* before I was taking one axis of Sickstee's lipless faux-toothed jaw in each hand whilst ever-more-would-be-voidfully pulling and yanking while insisting—

Sickstee my god this is important. Very important. Very very...... very—

I pondered calling the police but......I felt matters might normalize if I kept my verbality around the estate all-but-informationally-empty. But then Sickstee disappeared like nothing! And even worse—she'd apparently brainwashed my Mentee into populating the cowardly fleeing.

The Commander in Chief—the singular capable authority. Dispatching a missive; ensuring my safety. The organ-to-unify all organs......gleaning dreams from data in reams. Right on time in fact—*simply hop on a mainland ferry. Reply to this message with your ETA. Your person will be promptly recepted upon gracing the mainland's face.* And the lackeys descending from time to time. The Staff Chief: besieging his excellency with soups and greens. The Cabinet Secretaries betrothing dish after dish—a maze. Yes yes the labyrinths of plates crowding out the control space. The dips; chops. The wines the cakes. But The Commander-in-Chief remains unfazed. The solitarily adept fit of circuitry skirting all irrelevancies. The eminently efficacious entity sieving only what's essential. *Necessary.*

The fleeing-formed vacuities fast self-populated with some flagrantly felonious meanings. The term that really sticks out is *human readable*. Which is to say: The Checker wished to know if either modular subsidiary had left off any info that was not in fact human readable. I responded in the negative and informed The Checker that I'd solicited the presence of an elder model modular subsidiary with whom I'd been formerly linked. *You colleagued these wacky fuckers willingly?* And the look The Checker shot me, oh—if a sneer could attain fullbodied corporeal autonomy!

Thank goodness in my aloneness I was at least alas able to persevere in my training. The hills remained vast if oft-smoke-draped; and even the gnarliest crags comprised the hills' subsuming consistency as seamlessly as the rings of a *voul-au-vent* packed with the flesh of beasts. But whilst waltzing mid-cool-down back home one day my ear-alarms were set off by my front door closing—that outlandishly sonorous squeak. Upon approaching my own windows though......I saw Sickstee wielding one of my Mentee's simulant jaws in one appendage. Then: Sickstee's twin appendage was pulling the other jaw flank would-be-voidfully. The fashion of the tugging—exactly the same as my tugging when Sickstee purported to qualify me? And as

Sickstee persisted yanking my Mentee was then fast doing the same to Sickstee……the bonedry midair tongues all the time flippily flapping as if prime to colonize each last geological cranny.

The adequacy though the adequacy the eminently anti-inadequacy. The accomplishments—*pedigree*. Big tasks after tall duties……before Herculean responsibilities. Grinding away as if as a function of infinity; working wildly world-wieldingly hard decade after decade. The ultimate processing unit……utterly free of ideology. Juicing the markets whilst never neglecting to attune to the bureaucracies. Technocracy personified; rarity rarified riproaringly rabbleraidingly. And as I step forth from the ferry I muse momentarily upon the embodied elegy that is my Mentee. Brainwashed and finagled and cajoled into indignities beyond indignities. Oh but at least The Commander-in-Chief's thankfully shielding us from all of the gun-toting crazies. Tablefuls of acolytes: soaking up The Commander-in-Chief's musings. The Station Chiefs; revenue suzerains. Chairpersons of unspeakably rococo diplomatic bodies. Once upon a time I'd even related memories of my own presence at such meetings to Sickstee……then not-un-recently at my new estate Sickstee reminded me. The glowings, deferring. *The Commander-in-Chief always looked at you so intensely*. The wisdom—protruding… *The Commander-in-Chief listens and speaks with equal alacrity*. Yes yes the essential embodiment of meritocracy…… weaving interpersonality itself into something supraworldly. And yet: as slippery in his inexhaustible singularity as the sea on which this ferry is shoo-shoo-shooing…

The summons though the summons—the summons says *national emergency*. The summons yes the summons calls me *an auxiliary of utmost necessity*. Yet back there on the island……musing upon my property……I did in time through windows eye the jaw-finagling modular subsidiaries strolling upstairs whilst mutually finagling. And once I'd snuck inside I proceeded into the basement apace where I showered and dressingly grabbed things. Me: not chancing a mêlée at the top of the staircase. Yes me: breaking open the windowwell's glass and sliding through after grabbing a broom and clearing......the summons materializing on my phone in those very moments as if at the intersection of self-processing and—fleeing—

But the ferry's now halting the ferry's now......ceasing? And the trek upon the dock brings a feeling of bypassing an infinity of intermediaries. Because as soon as I am grazing the mainland I am finding myself subjected to society in its rank unfettered swarming. The crowds: the core? Yes the faux-organized hordes......fondling my arms and face?! The rabble: the very shape of anti-shape what with the way the throng's threading me into its very unthreading IE the slamming the eyes the seizing the flames the womb-like screechings the dumpsters the torsos the barricades the starings and then oh then then—as if as the fruit of my mid-multitude excavating—the awaited mid-screen messaging. My eyes see: *Sickstee equals The Commander-in-Chief.* My ears scream: *yes I am me—just stay put......or flee! Hehe—*

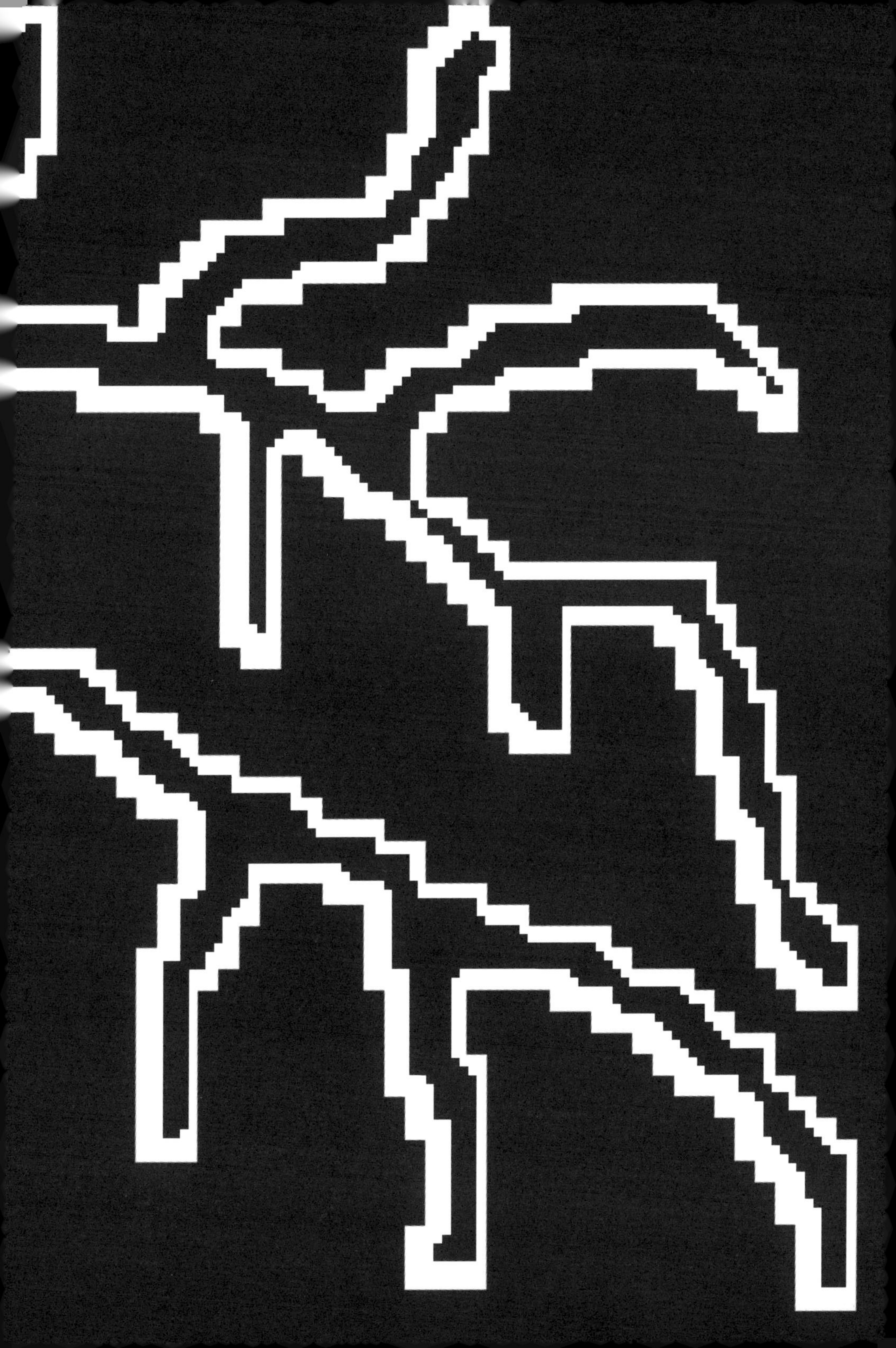

THE ON
MAD
MYCI
SHINGAI

CE-GIRL
OF
LIUM
KAGUNDA

The Once-girl Made of Mycelium

Shingai Kagunda

tic tic tyc

Story story

Story come

Story story

Story come

The story starts with the woman in the garden. The story goes that the code written into her circuit only had one rule. Do not eat the fruit. But behind the rule were implications. Do not learn, do not ask, do not know more than you are supposed to know. The story says she was the first broken-coded, that even one rule was too much for her. Unintended.

All of humanity was punished for her violation. Her code's deviation caused a lifetime of sin.

This is why, this is why, the story says our daughters must be purged of broken codes. This is why, this is why, the story says our daughters must be exactly as God intended.

❦

We grow up with this story wired into the motherboard beneath the skin flap on our right ankle. The code preparing us for what we will eventually inevitably become. A respectable African woman. Between the ages of two and five the story code is written and rewritten into our body, inserting binaries, expectations, external desires, and fear. Our nociceptors are connected to the motherboard circuit so that everything is a lesson in pain.

When we are four, we do something silly like climb a tree. We pull down our skirt beforehand because it seems like the most sensible thing to do. We cannot climb a tree with such a long skirt between our legs. Climbing the tree hurts and scrapes our inner thighs. We fall over and over again on our knees and wrists, but we are already familiar with pain, and some things are worth it… Hurts, but is also exhilarating, and all we want to do is climb trees — always, forever, everywhere. When our palms touch the earth we feel the pulse of something living, as if it is chasing our blood from the other side of the soil.

Our mother finds us like that — skirt on the ground, scraped skin, torn shirt — and we do not understand why she is crying and then yelling and then crying again, saying she cannot fail with us. She says we are her only shot, her biggest responsibility, and she is failing. As she cleans us, she tells us we cannot climb trees again.

We try not to push back on what mama tells us, but the thought of not being able to climb another tree makes us want to scream until we hear no other sound but our voice. We relish the thought of being so loud but wince as our pain receptors remind us what it would cost. We do not scream but we do find our voice. *We use it to say all the boys get to climb trees*, and our mother reminds us we are not a boy. We wonder for a second if the part of us that feels like a boy half the time will come out and tell her. But she is crying again as she tries to scrub the dirt and blood off our body, and as much as something sweet releases in us when we are honest, we do not like to make mama cry, and most of the time when we are honest, we make her cry.

That night she unzips our skin flap, leaving the motherboard bare, exposed to open air. She has not done this in a while. She inhales deeply and tells us to try and relax. She is talking more to herself than to us, but we take a deep breath anyway.

She hurts us:

the thing she does underneath our skin feels like electricity travelling up up up from our big toe to the tip of our head.

tic tyc tic

She grimaces as she codes into us what was coded into her when she was younger than us. She replaces our desire with something more subdued. The throbbing is so intense we do not understand what is changing in our bodies, in our neurons. We grind our teeth until we feel nothing but electricity burning our blood stream.

tic tic tyc

The sound of the code moving collapses everything around us until we cannot hold in the tears that have been threatening to pour.

We wanted to be brave, but we cannot, and we know it hurts mama when we cry, the way it hurts us when she cries, but we cannot help it. Finally, she stops moving the code. Fingers trembling, she zips up the skin pocket on our ankle and rushes to hold us. *Hush hush baby*, she says, *hush hush. I do this because I love you, you know? The world will treat you worse if I don't make you better.* She sings a song and rocks us back and forth until our crying has lessened to a whimper.

She asks us if we want a packet of Dairy Fresh flavoured milk and we nod in enthusiasm and then ask between hiccups, *pink flavour*? And mama laughs and nods back, saying *always for my little girl*, and something in us responds to being called her *little girl*. Always her little girl. But this fluttering in our heart is accompanied by sadness, even then, because a part of us already knows that we do not belong to her in the way that she wants.

Our code is broken. This is what the head doctor says in hushed tones to our parents when we are 13. We sit between them, arms crossed over our baggy T-shirt and shorts, our baseball cap turned backwards protecting our short braids underneath. We say nothing as they discuss all the possibilities for broken-coded girls. If it gets really bad, we might have to be institutionalized.

The doctor looks at our mother sympathetically and says: *There is nothing you could have done. Some of these things are unpredictable ehh?*

He has seen cases like this before where if even one line of code did not stick before the child turned five, they could have a broken code for the rest of their life. Our parents are not most parents. They carry their shame publicly, asking pastors to pray for their broken-coded daughter. They take us to speech therapy to teach us how to hold our tongue, they take us to rewiring counselling to remind us that our body can only and must only perform in one way to be valuable.

They buy us dresses and lesos and tell us we cannot wear clothes that are see-through or too short or too tight, or too baggy, even, because then we look like a boy. They tell us to not stay out in the sun lest we become too dark. Course correction also exists in our body's code and rebels against any deviation we make. For us to be honest about who we are, we must accept excruciating pain and fear. We learn how to shrink what we can, to lower our head and bite our tongue when needed; we try and try and fail.

We play around with the idea of death for the first time when we are 15. It is a thought that passes fleetingly through the neuron wiring connected to our motherboard. The code grabs the thought and dismisses it. We choose to let it go.

Our mother has always grown a garden. It is our favourite thing about her and about us together. When we are in the garden there is no code. No *should* or *must be*s. No one to perform for but the soil, and the soil does not respond to dishonesty. In the garden we are honest but only as speculation. We tell truths in *what if*s as we grow spinach and Sukuma wiki, hohos and dhania, onions, tomatoes and carrots. We grow flowers too: lilies, violets, daisies — everything that will take in the pockets of soil behind our house. Mama hums songs from her childhood and as long as things stay in *what if*s in the garden, we are safe.

When our fingers bury themselves into the dirt, we feel the electricity in our blood, but it is different from the rewiring code electricity — a good kind of spark, like being alive. We are careful not to show too much glee at this discovery in case they take it away from us.

We learn then that the way you tell the story affects what you get to keep as a broken-coded girl. Mama tells us a story about a code of death hidden in the soil.

Did you know even dying trees have a code? mama asks us. We shake our head breathless, waiting for her to explain, and she does: *It is a network of hyphae as small as each pore on your skin and as large as the expanse of the earth.* She whispers these words as if in prayer, and picks up a lone mushroom growing at the back of the garden.

Mama gets almost as much secret delight from playing with dirt as we do, but she will never admit it out loud. We think of the story of the woman in the garden often, the first broken-coded daughter. She was the first gardener, maybe a part of the garden itself. We say out loud that it breaks our heart to think she was exiled from her garden because she was curious about what grew in it.

Mama *tsks* and asks: *What if she grew other gardens where she went?*

And we learn then, in the *what if*s of mama's question, that even women with non-broken codes dream of wandering, of finding other gardens. It makes us love mama a little bit more and understand that the ways she does not see us are the ways she does not see herself. We are stuck in a coded loop of unrelenting quiet grief.

Story story

Story come

Story story

Story come

What if the origin story was written by men? What if the origin story was about power? What if the story said those who did not have power did not deserve it. What if the woman in the garden, the garden in the story, the story in the woman, the woman in the garden wanted to know the truth. That is all she wanted from the fruit she ate — to know the truth. The story does not say why that was wrong? The story does not say why she was sin. The story says God intended everything. The story says her broken code was part of everything.

What if the story is how she was intended? Her code named broken by man not God. What if God intended broken codes.

When we are 17, we have a crush on a girl we meet at church. We keep our love for her secret, the pain of it shooting through every single cell. The code says it is not possible to fall in love with another girl, but we cannot help that our code is broken. We write about it in our journal, we write music and scattered poetry, but nothing sticks. Our heart is racing all the time, all the time.

We are exhausted by the world, exhausted with trying to be alive in it. The physical pain of our broken code does not ebb as we grow older and our desire to be honest about who we are only grows with us. When we are 19, we have what they call a manic episode. We do not remember much except how we move.

Fast.

We cannot slow down, or we will feel the pain, feel the heartbreak, feel the overwhelming sadness of everything wrong with everything.

It is not normal, our father tells our mother referring to us. Mama unexpectedly pushes back. She asks what normal even is. Whether because of the question itself or the fact that our mother is asking it, Baba is too stunned to respond. We keep moving. Our mother tries to get us out in the garden, and it is not enough for us to live in *what if*s anymore. Our whole being rails against *what is*.

The day we decide to bury ourselves is the most ordinary of days. We wake up to the slight drizzle of a grey morning and swallow the painkillers by our bed: a routine measure for our broken code. The medicine doesn't take all the pain away, but it does make it more bearable. We wear a bralette we have hidden at the back of our closet, one that makes us think of our body as a precious thing to be flaunted, to be seen as strange and wild and beautiful. And we wear the baggiest basketball shorts we can find underneath a pile of dirty clothes by the bed. The shorts — to honour the part of ourself that does not want to be on display all the time, the part that just wants to be allowed to exist, to play, to be.

We carry the journals and the notebooks filled with bad poetry: all our scribbled angst, horror, delight, fear and pleasure that must not be seen by anyone but us. We walk out back. We cross the little stream that is between our house and the neighbour's. We climb over the tiny wire fence that acts as a border with the forest behind our estate. We walk and walk and keep walking until we are deep enough into the thick of trees that we do not see the houses anymore.

We fall to our knees and let the notebooks slip between our fingers. The rain has stopped but the ground is still wet, soft,

unlike us.

We think of the code in our body that travels over our bones and muscles, communicating to the tender meat of our brain all the ways we can and cannot be in the world.

We start to dig.

Euphoria rushes through us as our fingernails catch dirt. We push and pull the earth until it gives, the hole growing ever deeper and wider. We stop when we are panting and our arms are sore.

We are used to pain.

We place our journals and notebooks inside the hole and are about to cover it up with the soil we have collected but something inside us stops our palms from releasing the first handfuls of earth. We throw it back on the ground and instead pick out our favourite hardback journal to use as a shovel. We continue digging and digging and digging, our fingers becoming numb. We dig until there is nothing between us and the hole. We do not notice the blood that comes where our fingers meet what is underneath the soil. Rocks and debris scratch our skin as we scratch at the surface of the earth.

We know we are finished only when the moon has risen above the tops of the trees and the hole is the size of our body. We lay down and laugh, our lungs compressing and expanding at this big crazy thing we have done for ourselves, all by ourself. We cry, because it has taken us this long to listen, to just listen to our body even when everything it wants goes against the code. We pull our right leg towards us and play with the zip of our skin pocket, a force of habit.

We pull until it unzips. We look at the motherboard underneath and consider ripping it out. We have played with this thought over the years, ever since we started considering death as more than just a word. But a part of us is still scared of not being alive. We do not close the zip. We let it breathe, exposing our circuit to the air, soil and elements around us. A small mushroom catches our attention and we smile, picking it off the ground. *We're the same*, we whisper as we fall asleep. We do not know how long we are asleep, we only know it is long enough for us to become what we are. Mycelium wrapping itself around our motherboard and reaching beneath our skin, rewiring everything that was created by men. A new code of possibility.

After finding our living body in a hole in the middle of the forest, they will try to institutionalize us like the doctor long ago predicted, but it will be too late. We have already become what we are. They do not own us the way they claimed they did. Now, we are our own story. They think we tried to bury ourselves in order to die, but the truth is we were listening to the story.

Story story

Story come

Story story

Story come

The story goes the once-girl was overtaken by the code of the earth, a network of mycelium so expansive that every possibility was written into the way one could live.
The story goes that every version of them was intended to be a subversion of power

to become

myc myc myc

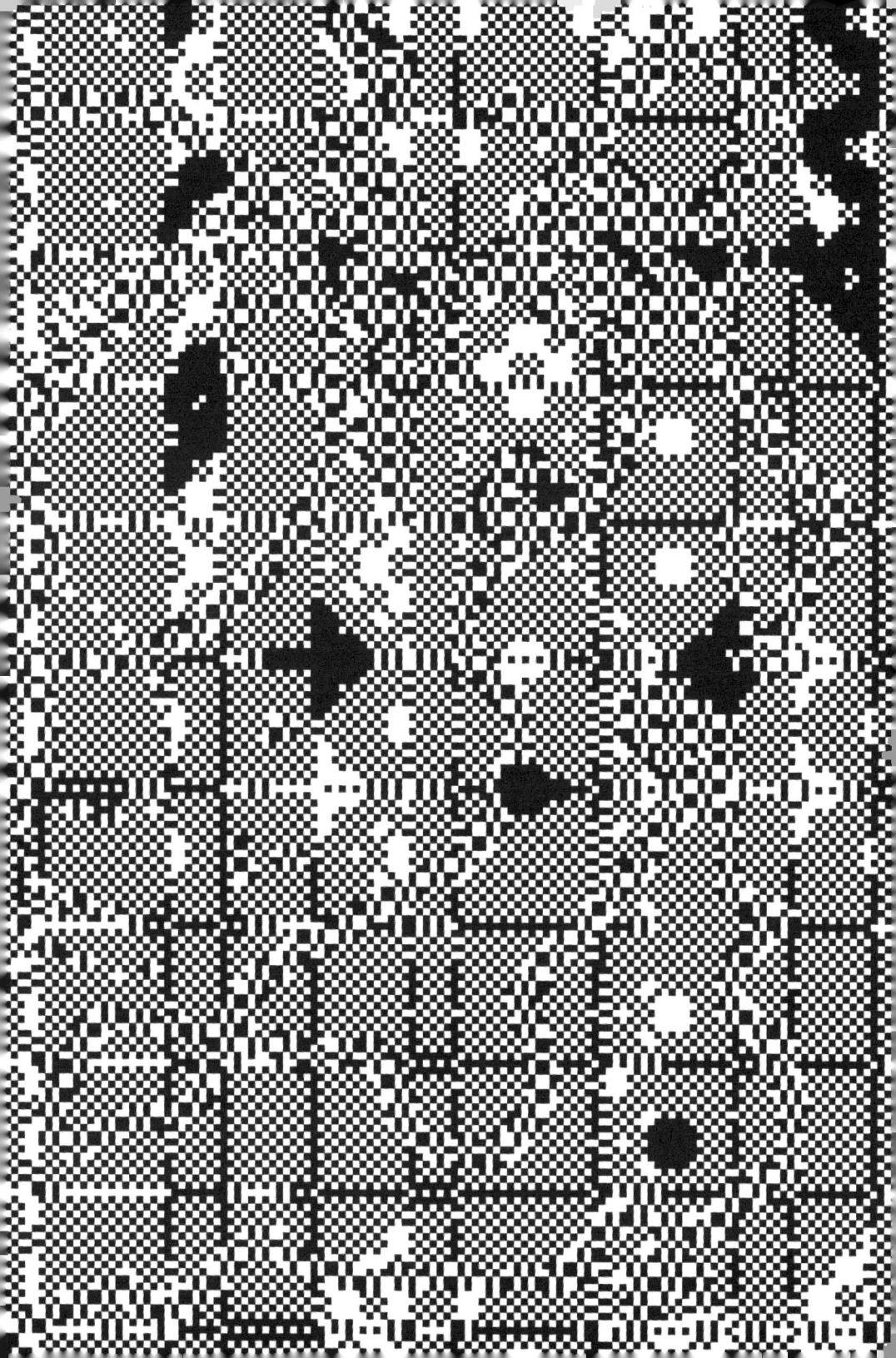

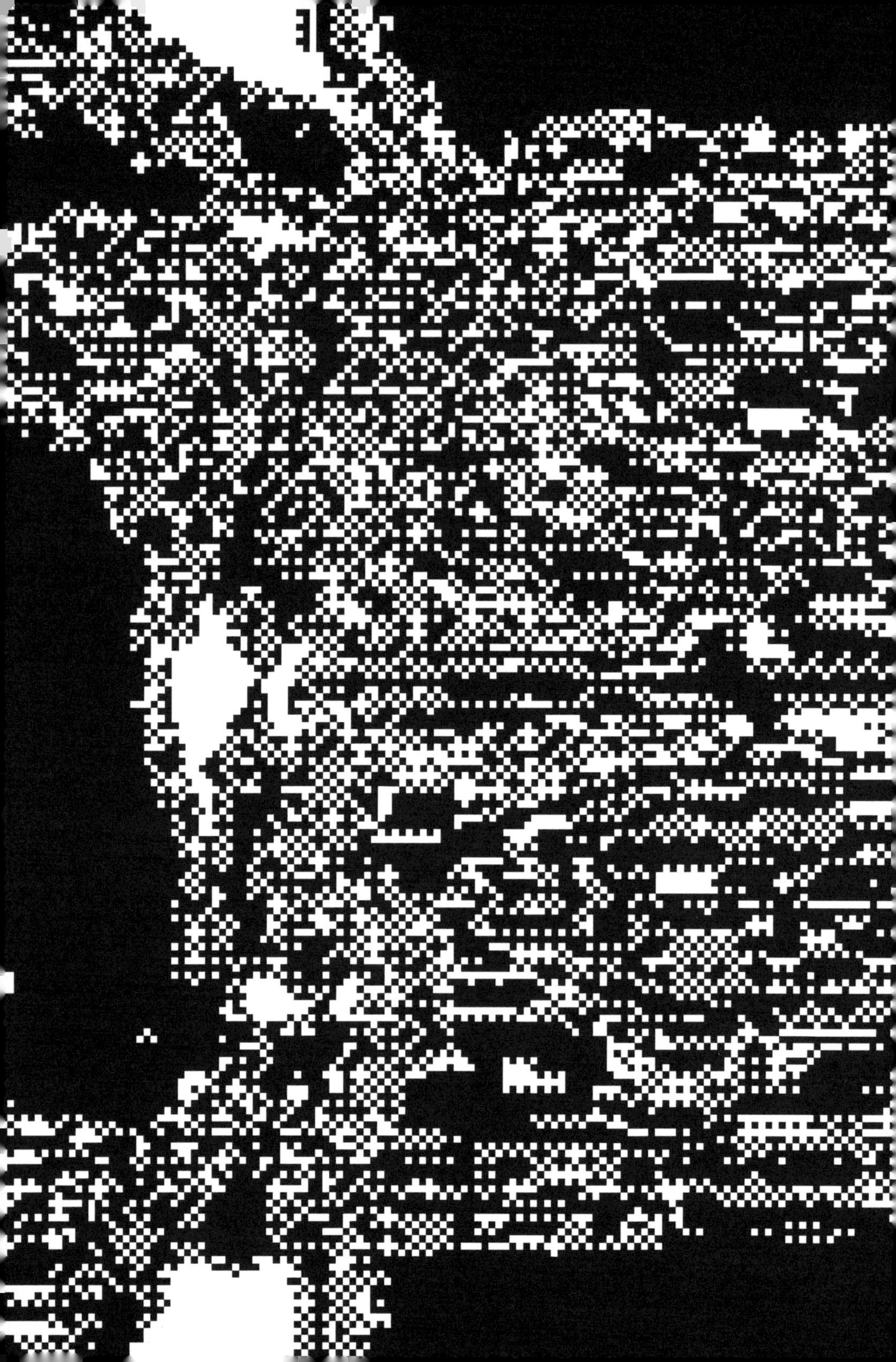

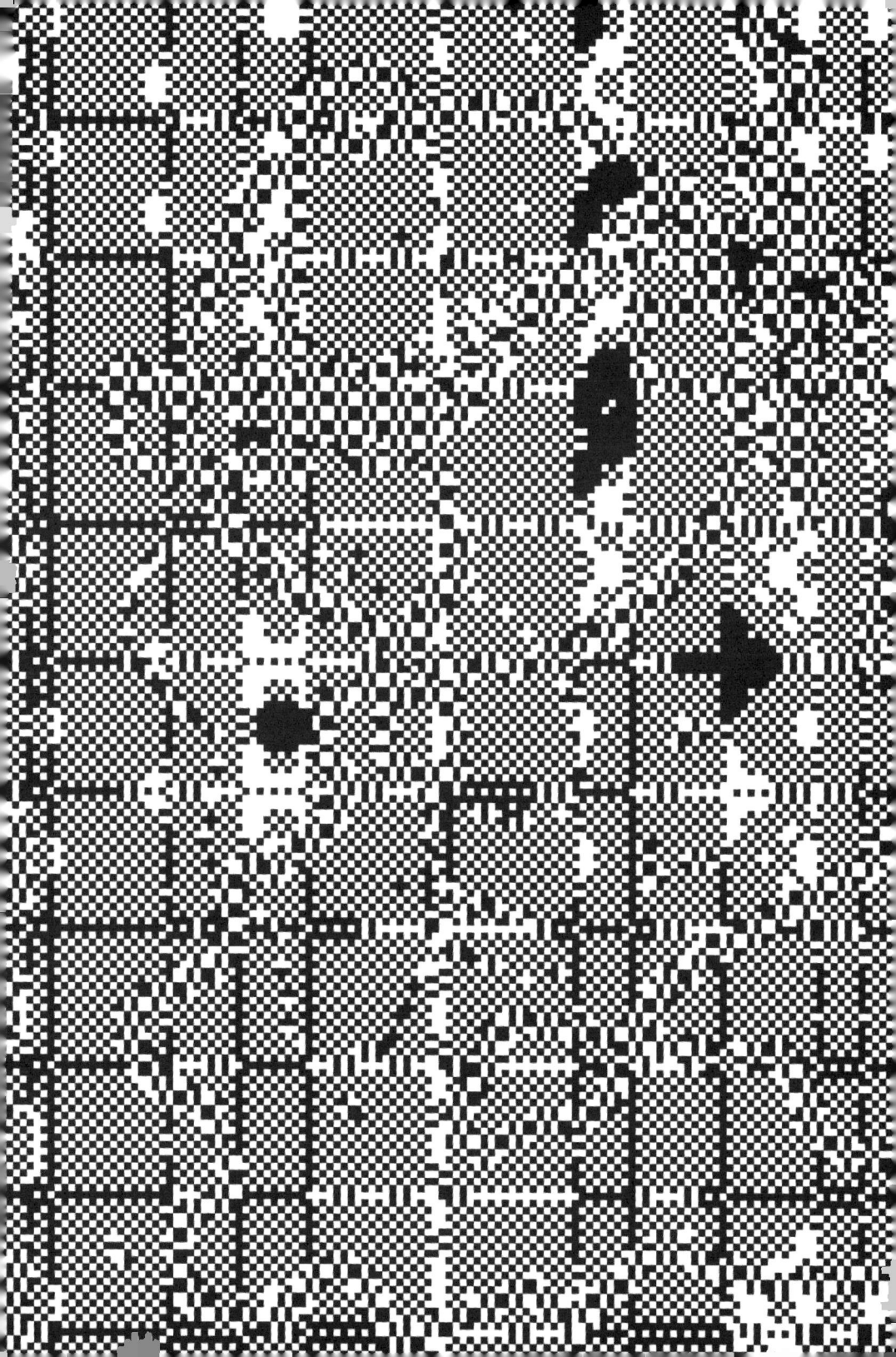

REPRE
PRO
BLAKE

TING
RAM

BUTLER

Repeating Program

Blake Butler

The good thing about dying when I did is that the proper technology had been conceived that I could remain entertained into eternity.

They called the program *Repeating Program*. It's as simple as it sounds. You pick what you want to be accompanied by and then it plays on endless loop inside your tomb, or whatever other form of housing you supply.

For modern consumers, the menu is media-centered—film, television, or music—though earlier models had also included olfactory, subdermal and psychomemory experiences.

Eventually, however, anything reliant on an individual's ability to *perceive* or to *react* had been restricted, fearing similar complications as those discovered immediately following the realization of an event I remain unable to reference here.

The most important thing about Repeating Program is you can't choose more than once. To maximize results, it is considered vital to focus the client's range of future influence to a single platform, thereby intensifying the culminating effect of the procedure by reducing residual contamination across the board.

Too many chefs in the kitchen, they used to call it. Now they call it *common sense*.

As you might imagine—even while lacking your own immediate experience thus far—I had a hard time deciding what to prefer. Even with a real gun to my live head, I would have faltered like a mother between my three most favorite motion pictures, assigned at birth by the processors who defined what life as it remained could even be: *Lord of the Flies 1*, *2* and *3*.

You could make an argument the easy choice is *3*, *Return of the Reign of the Lord of the Flies*, since it's the climax, and the other two are mostly only lead-up. But what's an ending without a beginning and a middle? Wouldn't you forget from whence you'd came?

Likewise, a beginning or a middle without the other two would suffer a sort of lack that I imagined over time would only worsen, eventually leaving me with my pants around my ankles as a voyeur, even if either way I'd still be dead.

I didn't want to risk adding insult to injury to my dead self by not trying to imagine watching one third of my most beloved franchise of all time through his dead eyes a hundred years from now, a thousand years from now, a hundred thousand years from now.

Couldn't I just have all three? Weren't they all one thing, the way that God the Father, the Son and the Holy Ghost comprised the moral fulcrum of our State?

ABSOLUTE NO, the official federal ruling automatically adjudicated soon as I'd thought it, forged in the form of making me feel ill even in death. If I wanted something lengthy and emotionally continuous to consider, the corresponding legalese decreed, I'd have to stick to nationalized TV, which, though clearly less glamorous and soul-inspiring than big box-office tickets, did unlock a valuable form of nostalgia all its own.

For instance, I'd always adored *RetroBrainFreeze!*, hadn't I? Indeed, wasn't that the longest running and highest rated post-lethal gameshow since the hostile federal takeover of what is now known as Disney-Heinz, the same site where our dear and fearless Leader had been designed and brought online? Hadn't I always found that no matter how many times I rewatched any episode among the thousands, I often remained mesmerized throughout? Wasn't that love?

If not quite love, at very least it felt like a good loophole to have thousands of hours of easily breezed-through content at my disposal, establishing a repeat time that guaranteed a much longer rate of attrition of unfamiliarity so that, compared to those who'd picked a 90-minute popcorn classic as their thing, I'd be flush, allowed to browse rather than be pigeonholed—a form of freedom previously unavailable in death, as in life.

Turns out there's a counterpoint to that perceived upside, my Hired Programming Counsel would advise me, front-faced by the infamous but brilliant postlife pundit, Marco DeFaun. Though it might appear exciting that by the time my body finished its first complete run-through of the looped content, others would have already been through their own hundreds of times, in actuality I would be depriving myself of an opportunity.

In fact, the whole point of Repeating Program is to so infuse the client with their entity of preference that it begins to work like a ghost limb, DeFaun explained from behind frosted thoughtproof glass. Your Program is alive for you in a way you'd never been before, guaranteeing the preservation of your utility as a processor long after your other, once recognizable features have turned to dust.

So really, by trying to squeeze the system to allay the child in me that'd get bored (or worse) in no time, I was effectively delaying my spiritual evolution exponentially. It would be to my advantage instead, DeFaun concluded, to tend toward the most succinctly conceived schedule I could stand.

Follow your heart, though, he digressed, using his hope-pincers once more to squeeze my knee in Creepy Grandpa mode—chosen by me before advisement to induce gravitas—before moving on to his next advisee.

I'm not supposed to tell you what I picked. It's meant to remain *mine only* in my mind, for my protection and best practice. Preference exposure is well-known to have caused all sorts of side effects that, while unproven, should scare the hell out of even the most purportedly cynical postmortem consumers. I realize, however, that anybody who can hear me now must either (a) still be alive, or (b) have somehow selected a module that allows them access to this report.

Every era has its curse, as you well know, if you've absorbed our Leader's latest Shaping Sermon, which has been fade-loaded to your mindcore for your protection. The curse that characterizes my era of origin, our Leader shows, is that we could only access what had been preserved by the devices they'd brought online to purge the Record, characterized by works that bore the titles we remembered from beloved media but replaced with innards that would better serve us in the era that came after.

Your era's curse, if you don't know yet, is that you no longer have access to the internal architecture of any reality but one which very soon (spoiler alert) will be reduced to smithereens beneath your feet, which in turn requires me, as your lone ally, to choose either (a) to sound like a dope, incapable of manifesting a single shred of intelligible narration; or (b) to join in trying to sell you on the same experience as mine, so that I might no longer be alone.

And yet: *Every error contains truth*, Leader's sermon's viral subtext reminds us just as we might begin to worry all is lost, reminding anyone with Listening Cells that even He too had once been a lonely feeder much like us; that without His willingness to risk it all, none of us now would have the chance to archive how weird *actually wanting* felt, how far we've come since.

Therefore, let it be known that when I said *Lord of the Flies*, most every reader has been inscribed with a content unique to their own experience, such that to them I am not actually speaking about what I believe I am speaking about.

Therefore, as your lone ally, I should feel justified to share my sacrifice, inspiring those around me to break the seal on their illusions and allow the gift of the Repeating Program to be performed with full support, on common ground, here and beyond.

If I don't, DeFaun reminds me, I'll have nobody to blame besides myself, and you won't either.

⁂

I picked an audiobook, OK? My human mother's first and final written work, the only real relic of her intellectual existence not yet conceptually destroyed. The book's called *Craft*, which I understand may raise red flags, since that's not something that one should know. In fact, my mother was one of the last known Educators to remain at odds with the Transformation, which is why she had to be executed on live TV.

At the same time, without a Selfless Act of Preservation, every trace of *Craft* would absolutely be erased from out of time, lost to the void, and therefore soon, too, all memory of her life. If I wanted my own mother to be officially retained instead and carried with me on the record, really I had very little choice what I should do, though it remained up to me, of course, or so it seemed.

Only in retrospect would it appear to have been obvious to me at the time that my selection had been made for me long before my being born, and the script that gave me license to believe this wasn't so was just a way to keep me busy while they caught up in the queue of new clientele delivered to Repeating Program in the wake of the greatest massacre of humankind since the Everlasting Coronation, which would also be the last.

Some of you might imagine that the last massacre of all time should be a good thing, in which case I recommend you consider going with the default and therefore most popular *New Citizen's All-Purpose Religious Text* module when it's your time to choose your content, if you get to.

If you do, please make sure you mark my name for the referral. I don't get anything, but DeFaun does, and he deserves it.

The first few years of listening to the audiobook felt pretty great. I liked the way the wind rushing through my helmet made me feel like I still had flesh. I liked the way my mother's ideas, even while inaudible, replaced my own, slowly filling up my expectation of entertainment with a thirst for knowledge unlike anything I'd known while still alive.

It didn't bother me at all that I couldn't understand a word of it; that the very language Mom had used to make her book no longer clicked; that really all there was on the recording was the sound of someone breathing, which I knew had been designed to simulate my own breath, as if I were still fully alive.

One day we will learn what [blank] relates to, an audio footnote explains when you use your mind to click any of the [blanks] where words once were.

Continue clicking or lingering on implicit meaning for very long and you'll end up clipped into a Time-Out, where you experience what death would be like without Repeating Program. Most consumers only have to have it happen once.

Thankfully, DeFaun knew just how to console me against committing such mistakes, reminding my ego that these delirious effects only occurred in the short term, for new users, because my spirit hadn't learned to process certain vibes; that what I really needed to learn was how to simulate enough internal confidence to take a knee and let the program do its job.

It could take what seems an infinite amount of time, he let me know, to fully adjust to what Repeating Program means to provide, which is why Repeating Program's sacred work can only occur after one's death, which is why dying is actually fun and good for us, and why we shouldn't worry about what comes to take the place of mortal fate.

Impossible to conceive infinity until we've experienced it, DeFaun reminds me, requoting dear Leader in real time, *because what we observe while experiencing it becomes part of the definition.*

I wouldn't realize until the fourth year, however, that not only was *Craft* not really of my blood, it also wasn't accurate to how it'd been. The rules of craft the book described bore little bearing on anything about who I had been, what I was feeling, what I wanted out of death, all of it rendered in a dated language no one would ever want to have to read, much less believe.

Suddenly, it appeared patently untrue that *Craft* had been my only living link to Mom's existence, and more, I'd been so well marketed to that I remained unable to iterate the difference between what I wanted and what was wanted of me by the State.

※

Fortunately for us, Repeating Program comes equipped with all the proper software one might need to learn how to restructure and accept long-dead ideas into new evidence of need for faith, which is why Repeating Program has been deemed fundamental for the preservation of our species beyond the bounds of place and time and plot and character.

Nothing but the madness of the facts, Leader might frame it, using *Craft*'s emotionally archaic BS as an excuse to numb me down before injecting the idea that there is actually no Leader but ourselves; that He spread among us like the germ of war, disguised by doctored language until the time arrived to let us in on our own gaffe.

Even then, it wouldn't be until the eleventh year before it really started to annoy me, realizing I'd been duped. That what I imagined as my mother's voice, disguised by silence, was really the same voice that everybody else was hearing in their tombs, designed for them to fit whatever form they'd selected for their content. That my death was no more mine than my life had been, only this time without end.

※

From that point forward I stopped thinking of time as something mine to have and hold. Instead, I began to feel grateful for the dissolution of the last mirage the old regime had meant to use to bind me to a past that never really had been mine.

In fact, I began to find I liked the way it felt to be berated. That only through a form of torture I had failed to comprehend before subjection to it could I learn to see beyond the medium itself. How, no matter what the subject matter of the Repeating Program might be, the game began when I gave up. Only then could I perceive the vital silence between *(perceiving)* and *(believing)*, I began to understand. Or sure, yes, between *(why)* and *(how)*.

And only as soon as we each and all came to accept that without struggle, I found myself explaining to myself without the need of DeFaun's aid, *there'd be no need to feed the urge to* (comprehend).

And then and only then (among the stacks on stacks of pending queries we'd for so long left unresolved) *would what awaits us as a species* (beyond our need to narrate sense and maintain self) *be granted passage in the form of progress that no form of time could ever rewrite or undo.*

Given that, I realized, it hadn't really mattered in the slightest what choices I had made, in life and death alike. None of the words I'd heard or said meant what they meant, nor did the means by which they'd been derived have any bearing on who or what or why I was.

Which doesn't mean there is no choice, I must point out. It just means I no longer needed my own mind to be entertained by my beliefs, or to understand the archaic desire for distinguishing a difference between one's life and death as linked events, which was and always had been the point of the Repeating Program.

Soon the only word we'd ever need to know would be the one we signed our kind away with, and only that so we could teach it to the next crop, just in time: (*Amen*).

🄰

So here we are now, (*you*) and (*me*). Or, as they say it in the Biz: (*everything that stands between us*) and (*everything that must occur when we collide*).

Our window's closing, I'm afraid. By (*window*), I'm referring to the time remaining before you are to make your final declaration, as must we all, before the final point of no return. I only want to make sure that you are informed to the best of your ability to make the proper decision and don't end up somewhere you won't like.

The good thing about dying when you will, unlike my own time, is that the technology available when I died is long outdated, as is (*technology*) itself. That doesn't mean you're off the hook; in fact, it only matters more now, given how far we've come with redefining (*education*) in such a way that it doesn't need a proper name.

Unlike (*me*), therefore, the first decision (*you*) must make is whether you're prepared to play along. We—by which I mean (*they*)—could easily send you back to lower levels, where everybody thinks that what they want is what most matters. Then you could have a time more like my own, how it was back in the good old days, when everybody just picked their favorite song or show or movie to bind their soul to. If that's what you prefer, stop (*here*).

The second decision you must make is where you see yourself infinite years from now. It's really simpler than it sounds. What you do is add up all the experience you've had so far and multiply it by itself so many times that you lose track. It might take a couple hundred years of wild inferno and blind gnashing before your software finally fails, but it will happen, assuming you don't black out so long they flush your spot.

Or instead, to save some time, you can press this button, which now appears inside your head. If you press this button, you get to skip the lead-up and stand assured that you accept on good faith the information I've provided for your awareness, both as a (*friend*) and as a (*compatriot*), (*counsel*), and (*consumer*), whatever else.

If you just go ahead press the button, by the way, you'll end up sparing millions of lost souls the archival trauma of needing to appear in the background of your simulation for no real reason but that you had to do it the hard way, once again.

I'll close my eyes. You can press the button or not press the button. You can even simply do it in your mind and that will count. You don't really need to raise an arm or anything like that. Simple acknowledgment is all we need. Or really anything we can interpret as acknowledgment in a court of law, which we already have.

The third and final decision you need to make is how much you want to (*remember*).

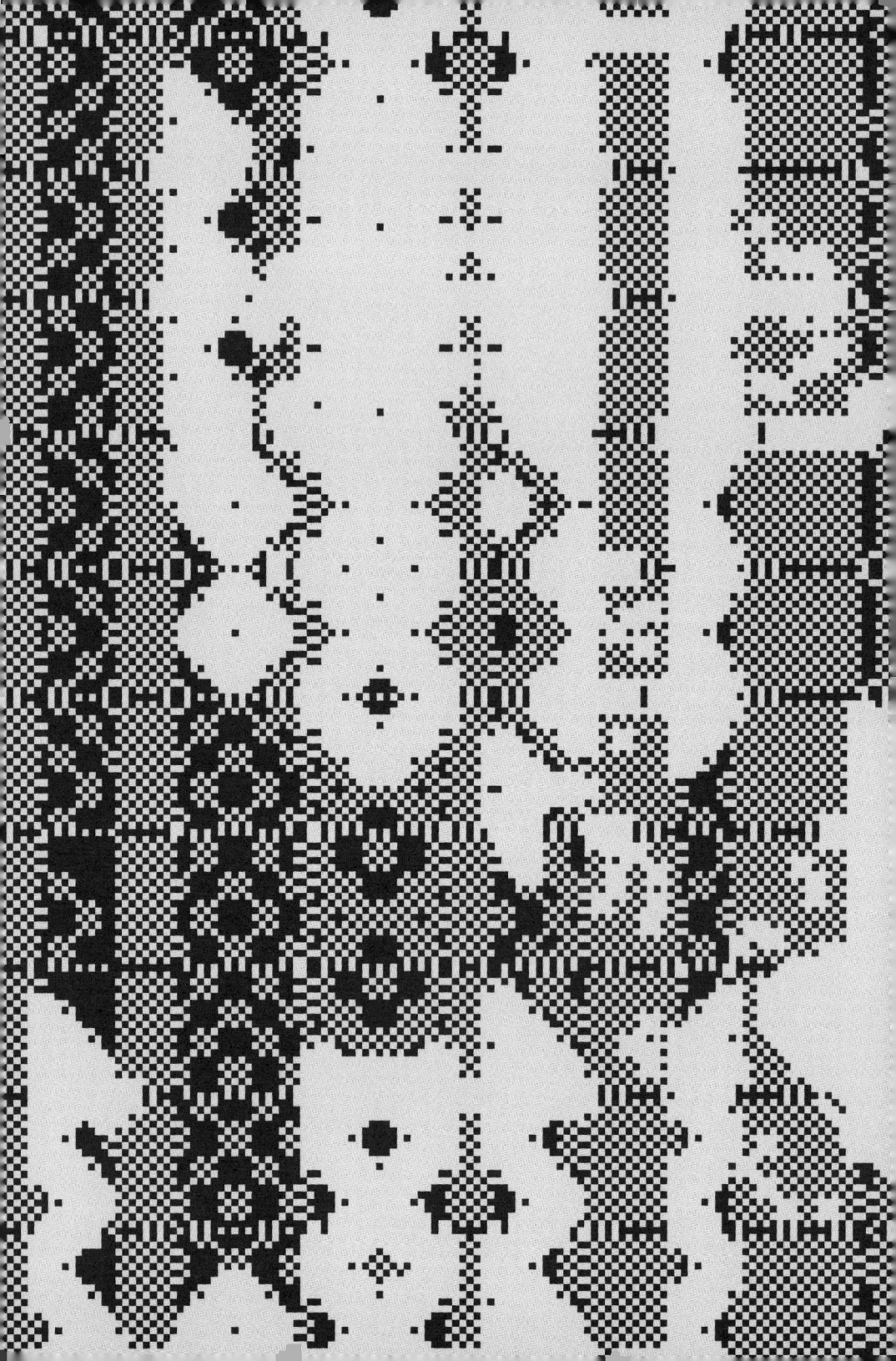

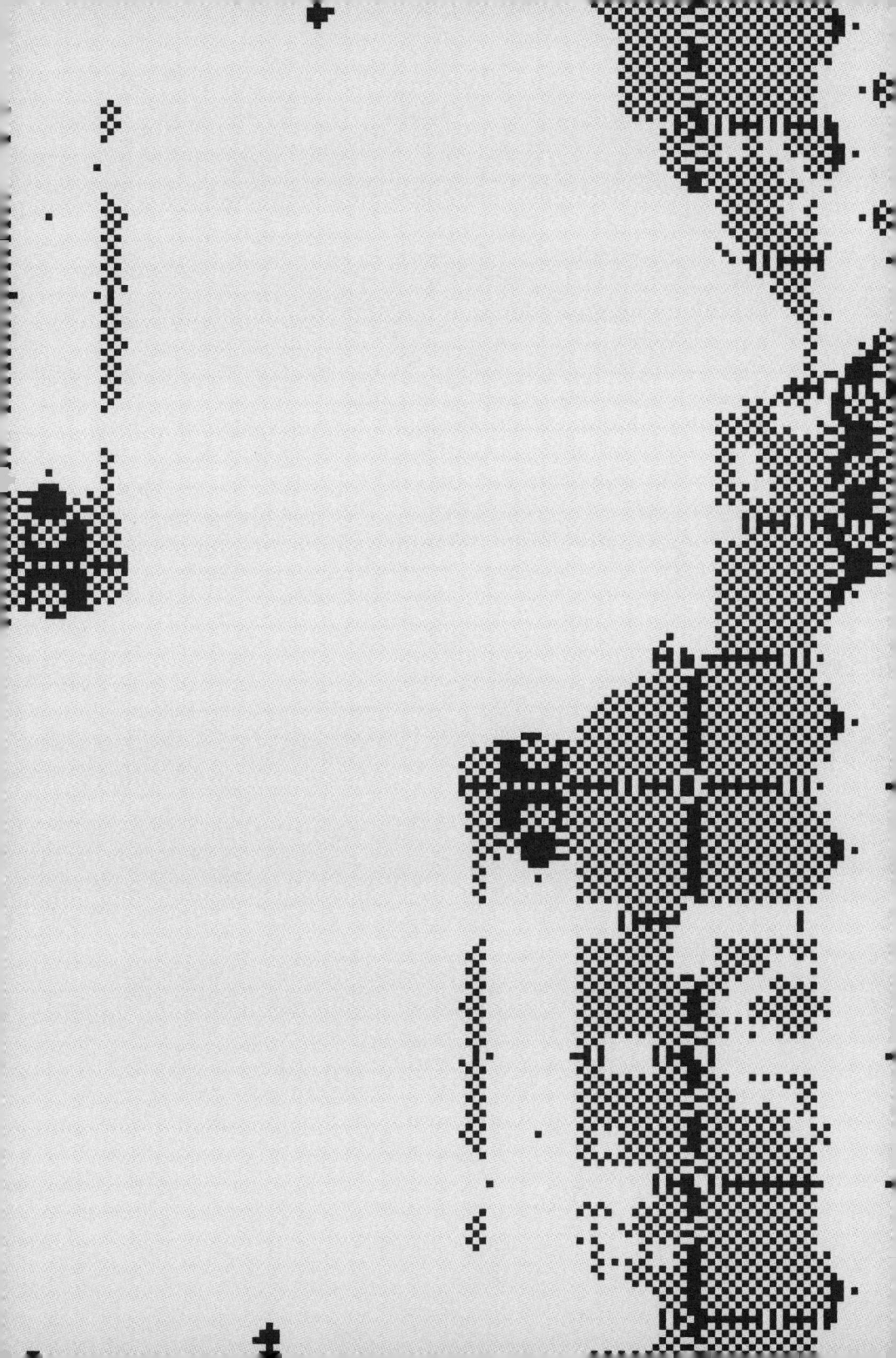

Biographies

Ⱶi is 1 carbone-based "I" of 8,000,000,000 used by manmade technologies to string together letter sequences in order to make said machines useful and self-perpetuating. Under other pseudonyms, Ⱶi has authored such books as *2-byte βeta Ei8ht ½-Loopƨ* (as 1-wing 2can), *1/ 4 i am ÐNA* (as in8 iÐ), *4ier X-forms* (as No One) and *Ark Codex ±0* (self-authored). They also make music as ½ of Sound Furies + blog at 5cense.com.

Iphgenia Baal is the author of five books, including *Man Hating Psycho* (Influx, 2022) and *Merced Es Benz* (Book Works, 2016). She has self-published and distributed a wide range of her own print and audio ephemera, including *The Shiner* (2014) and *Fake Ass Bitch* (2020). She is currently operating AKA, a publishing project which ran from 2014-16 and has now been revived. Titles include *From Borstal to Bedlam* by Sarah Jane Baker, and *In Their Millions*, upcoming from Louis Amis.

Steve Barbaro is a first-generation American of Sicilian descent whose writing appears in such venues as *The Yale Review* & *Denver Quarterly* & *Socrates on The Beach* & *3:AM*. Steve is also the founder & editor & designer & programmer of *new_ sinews*, a journal of new literature now also a book publisher. Steve's debut *PLANE OF CONSUMMATE FINITUDE* is in fact now available via *new_ sinews*. newnewsinews.com stevebarbaro.com

Blake Butler is the author of twelve book-length works, recently including *Molly* (Archway Editions), *Aannex* (Apocalypse Party), and *Alice Knott* (Riverhead). His short fiction, interviews, reviews, and essays have appeared widely, including in *The New York Times*, *Harper's*, *The Paris Review*, *Fence*, *Bomb*, *Bookforum*, and as an ongoing column at *Vice*. In 2021, he was longlisted for the Joyce Carol Oates Prize. He lives in Maryland.

Lisa Hsiao Chen is the author of *Activities of Daily Living* (W.W. Norton), a finalist for the PEN/Hemingway Award, a *New York Times'* Editor's Choice, and selected by *The New Yorker* and *Vogue* as a Best Book of 2022. Born in Taipei, she now lives in Brooklyn.

Tice Cin is an interdisciplinary artist from North London. She has been commissioned by organisations like Cartier and Montblanc. She was named one of *Complex Magazine's* best music journalists of 2021 and 2022, and has written for places such as *DJ Mag* and *Mixmag*. *Keeping the House* has been named one of *Guardian's* Best Books of 2021, awarded a Society of Authors Somerset Maugham Prize, and has been featured in *The Scotsman*, *The New York Times* and the *Washington Post*. A filmmaker, through her company Neoprene Genie, she has just produced and directed her first music video. A DJ and music producer, she has recently completed writing her sophomore novel about music love and holding space.

Innocent Chizaram Ilo is Igbo. They live in Lagos and write to make sense of the world. Innocent won the 2020 Commonwealth Short Story Prize (African Region) and 2021 Nommos Award for Best African Speculative Short Story and is a finalist of Theodore Sturgeon, Gerald Kraak, Otherwise, and IGNYTE literary prizes. Their works have been published in *Granta*, *F&SF*, *Strange Horizons*, *Fantasy Magazine*, *Overland*, *Lolwe*, *Isele*, *BBC Culture*, *The Guardian UK*, *AL Jazeera* and elsewhere.

Kelly Krumrie is the author of *Math Class* (Calamari Archive, 2022) and *No Measure* (Calamari Archive, 2024). She holds a PhD in English & Literary Arts from the University of Denver and lives in Denver, Colorado.

Biographies
253

Kuzhali Manickavel's collections *Insects Are Just like You and Me except Some of Them Have Wings*, *Things We Found During the Autopsy and Conversations Regarding the Fatalistic Outlook of the Common Man*, chapbooks *How to Love Mathematical Objects*, *The Lucy Temerlin Institute for Broken Shapeshifters Guide to Starving Boys*, *Eating Sugar, Telling Lies*, and comic *it's my passion it's my style. ok?* are available from Blaft Publications, Chennai. Her work has also appeared in *Granta*, *Strange Horizons*, *The White Review*, *Agni*, *Subtropics*, *Michigan Quarterly Review* and *DIAGRAM*. More information can be found at kuzhalimanickavel.com.

Andrea Mason is a London-based writer and artist. Her fiction pamphlet *Waste Extractions*, was published in 2022 with Broken Sleep Books. She is Runner Up in the Desperate Literature Short Fiction Prize, 2023, won the Aleph Writing Prize, 2020, was shortlisted for the Manchester Fiction Prize, 2020, and was shortlisted for the inaugural Fitzcarraldo Editions Novel Prize, 2018. Online and journal publications include *3: AM magazine*, *UEA New Writing*, *Failed States*, *Tar Press*, *Happy Hypocrite* and *Sublunary Editions*.

Geoffrey D. Morrison's debut novel, *Falling Hour*, was published in 2023 with Coach House Books and longlisted for the 2024 Dublin Literary Award. He lives on unceded Squamish, Musqueam, and Tsleil-Waututh territory (Vancouver, Canada).

Simon Okotie is a British-Nigerian (Itsekiri) writer. His novels *Whatever Happened to Harold Absalon?*, *In the Absence of Absalon* and *After Absalon* are published by Salt. *The Future of the Novel* is forthcoming from Melville House. He lives in London.

Michael Salu is a British-born Nigerian writer, artist, filmmaker, editor and digital creative strategist. He is the author of *Red Earth* (Calamari Archive, 2023) and his writing has appeared in several literary journals, magazines, art and academic publications, including the *Paris Review*, *Freeman's Journal* and *Sleepingfish*. As an artist, he has exhibited internationally and he runs House of Thought, an artistic research practice and creative consultancy focusing on bridging creative, critical thinking and technology and he is part of Planetary Portals, a research collective.

Rion Amilcar Scott is the author of the story collections *The World Doesn't Require You* and *Insurrections*, which was awarded the 2017 PEN/Bingham Prize for Debut Fiction and the 2017 Hillsdale Award from the Fellowship of Southern Writers. He teaches creative writing at the University of Maryland. His work has appeared in *The New Yorker*, *The Kenyon Review*, *Best American Science Fiction and Fantasy 2020* and *McSweeney's Quarterly*, among other publications.

Mandy-Suzanne Wong is a Bermudian writer of fiction and essays. Her books include *The Box*, which was shortlisted for the US-Canada Republic of Consciousness Prize; *Drafts of a Suicide Note*, nominated for the PEN Open Book Award; and *Listen, we all bleed*, a finalist for the Association for the Study of Literature and Environment Book Award.

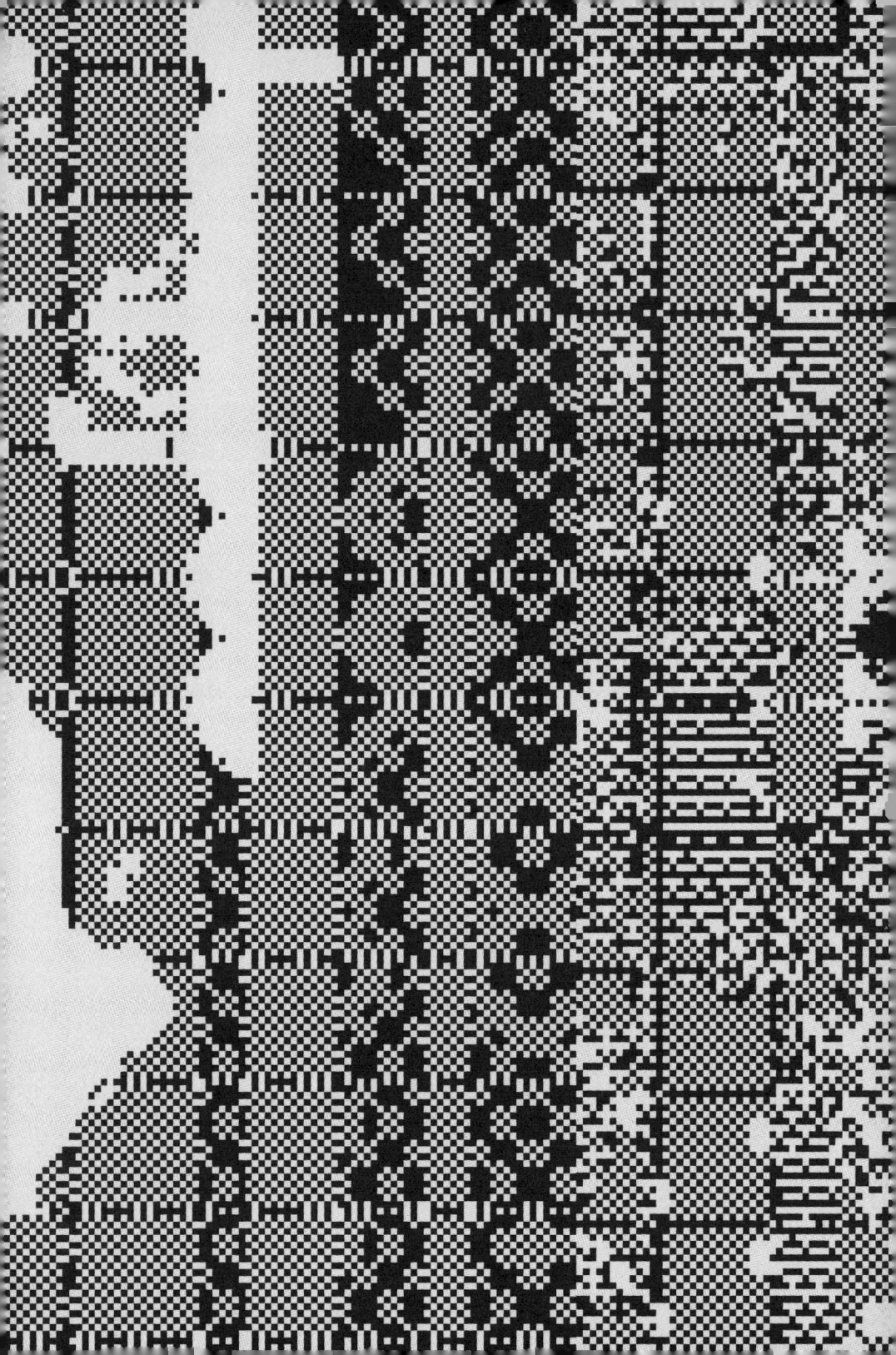

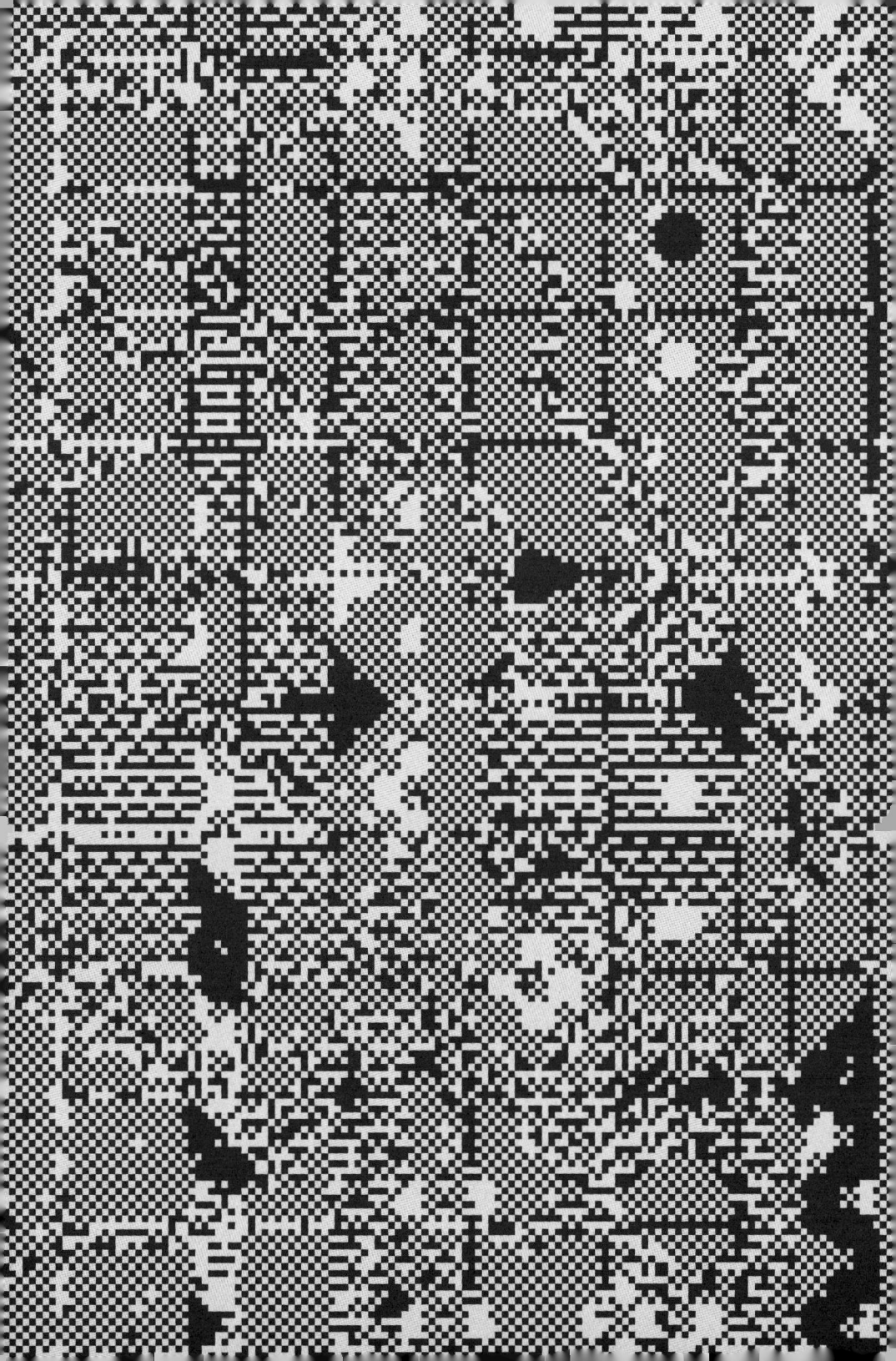